ENGLAND

Biographies and Acknowledgements

Ivan J. Belcher developed an interest in photography while serving with the RAF in India. On returning to Britain in 1949 he joined the Photographic Unit at Harwell, leaving in 1983 to establish his own successful colour picture library. He has spent the past few years travelling extensively throughout the country capturing all aspects of English life and culture.

For Stephen
Sonya Newland has lived in England all her life, and has spent much time in recent years exploring the country, indulging her joint passions for hill walking and English history. She now lives in London, but takes every opportunity to travel, particularly to the West Country and the Yorkshire Dales.

With grateful thanks to Helen Courtney who designed this book and to Anna Newland.

All pictures courtesy of Ivan J. Belcher except page 197 courtesy of
The Bridgeman Art Library.

This edition published by Barnes & Noble, Inc., by arrangement with Dempsey Parr

1999 Barnes & Noble Books

M 10 9 8 7 6 5 4 3 2 1

ISBN 0 7607 1605 6

First published in 1998 by DEMPSEY PARR
Queen Street House
4–5 Queen Street
Bath BA1 1HE

Copyright 1998 © Dempsey Parr

Produced for Dempsey Parr by Foundry Design and Production,
a part of The Foundry Creative Media Company Ltd,
Crabtree Hall, Crabtree Lane, Fulham, London, SW6 6TY

Printed in Korea.

ENGLAND

PHOTOGRAPHS BY IVAN J. BELCHER

Text by Sonya Newland

BARNES
& NOBLE
BOOKS
NEW YORK

Contents

Contents by Region

Introduction

I n no other country in the world does such geographical beauty combine with a long and illustrious history. England's past has left a legacy of rich cultural tradition, superbly mingled with contemporary life, that manifests itself in a wide variety of customs and beliefs, practised on both a local and a national scale. The English are a proud nation, and have long been one of the world's leaders in cultural, scientific, religious and political development, but it is their celebrated heritage of which they are most proud.

The first settlers in England were scattered Neolithic tribes who made homes for themselves in the caves along the coastlines and on the wild moors that provided the natural resources, such as water and building rocks, that were essential for their survival. Few prehistoric relics remain now to tell of the rituals and practices that characterised their lives, and those that do maintain an air of defiant mystery that challenges archaeologists and anthropologists to interpret their purpose and significance – the magnificent Stonehenge near Salisbury is the best-known and most remarkable of these.

The long line of kings and queens that England boasts is the most fascinating element of the country's great history. It is like a long and magical fairy tale, of wars and prosperity, revolution and suppression, power and weakness. Every English monarch has left a small but discernible mark on the land we see today. From the legendary King Arthur and his knights to the present Royal Family, the English monarchy is an enormous cast of very individual characters: the good, the brave, the cunning, the wicked and the downright mad, from heroes like Henry V to alleged villains like Richard III. In a

wonderful irony, Elizabeth I and Queen Victoria, both of whom ascended to the throne at times when women were regarded as less than intelligent than men, are two of England's most famous leaders, both reigning long – and supreme. It is this incredible tapestry of people and events that helps make England truly unique.

The Romans were the first race to establish themselves properly in England as rulers of the entire nation, and from them the English have an impressive legacy – one that tells of the Romans' long and turbulent dominance, not only over this small island, but over much of Europe as well. In the centuries following the decline of the Roman Empire, leadership of England was fought over bitterly by the Jutes, the Saxons and the Angles. The victorious Anglo-Saxons ruled for over six hundred years, despite continued attacks by the Danes, until Alfred the Great agreed a treaty that allowed the Danes to retain some of the land and both factions to live in peace.

The end of the period of Anglo-Saxon supremacy was decided at one of the most famous battles in English history: the Battle of Hastings. In 1066, Duke William of Normandy (later re-named William the Conqueror), landed with his armies at Hastings where a bloody battle raged until William emerged the victor over King Harold. The events of this battle are recorded on the immense Bayeaux Tapestry. Later, the House of Plantagenet replaced the Norman dynasty: Henry I's son drowned, forcing the king to make his daughter heir to the throne, and marrying her to Geoffrey Plantagenet. Some of England's most renowned monarchs reigned during this period and there was a revival of the old values of chivalry and honour. Wars were fought, but this time in the name of God, as Richard the Lionheart embarked on the series on missions known as The Crusades.

The Plantagenet House was brought down by Henry Bolingbroke, who later assumed the throne as Henry IV, and established the House of Lancaster. This period was dominated by the Wars of the Roses, when a senile Henry VI was forced to defend the throne against the Duke of York (the grandson of the Plantagenet king Edward III) who laid claim to the throne. Although York himself was killed at the Battle of Wakefield, his son Edward was victorious and was later crowned king of England. The House of York had a short and unfulfilled career as rulers of the land, despite Richard III's alleged efforts to secure his succession by murdering the young Edward V and his brother, the 'Princes in the Tower'.

The following Tudor period is best known for two of the most notorious monarchs in England's past: Henry VIII and his daughter Elizabeth I. This was a time of great reform – the Catholic church was abandoned on a whim of the temperamental Henry VIII, and the Anglican branch of Protestantism established. But while this was an era of great upheaval, it was also a time of great cultural advancement. The arts prospered, conquistadors discovered new lands, and English supremacy began to assert itself throughout Europe. This cultural affluence continued under the Stuarts, despite enormous religious and political problems, which included Guy Fawkes' famous Gunpowder Plot of 1605 and the Civil Wars.

From the early eighteenth century, England began to make its mark as a major world power: the Industrial Revolution made the country a leader in commercial affairs, and British success in the Napoleonic wars established the country as a force to be reckoned with on an international scale. By the time Queen Victoria ascended the throne in 1837, the British Empire was expanding rapidly.

England's recent history has obviously been dominated by the two World Wars. During this most turbulent time, the English sense of patriotism came to the fore, causing people to endure the hardships that came with such large scale conflict with a fortitude, courage and spirit that has characterised the nation for hundreds of years.

The relics of this long history are an integral part of the English landscape. A diverse, fascinating and immensely beautiful country, England's damp climate means that it is characterised by lush greenery. The hills and valleys are vibrant with flourishing plant life and ancient forests remain untouched homes to many species of wildlife. Along the craggy coastlines, seabirds nest in the crevices and amongst the dunes. Even in the cities, nature prospers between the modern developments, encouraged by the English love of beauty and greenery. Parks can be found in the heart of some of the busiest industrial areas, carefully planned and maintained, to provide colour amidst the grey of a winter's mist. In the coastal regions, long stretches of beach irresistably draw locals and tourists alike to savour the views and the atmosphere – if not always good weather.

Along these stretches, harbours and ports reflect England's fishing and other seafaring industries. For hundreds of years ports like Southampton and Portsmouth prospered as main bases for transatlantic travel, and docks like Liverpool and Chester drew their success from their trade links with Europe.

England's diversity of architecture is not only concentrated in the big cities. The country's capital, London, has a huge diversity of beautiful structures dating from all periods of history, and even some of the smallest villages contain buildings dating from centuries ago, particularly Norman times. These include parish churches, local manor-houses, bridges and, most frequently, cottages. In spa towns like Bath and Cheltenham, to name just two, the buildings exhibit a predominance of Georgian and Victorian architecture reflecting the rise in popularity of visiting the mineral springs and sea bathing during these periods. In other cities and towns, there are Roman walls, medieval houses and cobbled streets; these, mixed with styles from other eras, illustrate the growth and expansion of many small Roman or Saxon settlements to smart towns in their heyday during the nineteenth or twentieth centuries.

It is impossible not to fall under the spell of this small, but bewitching country, an area that has become representative of all that is noble, courageous and determined. All elements, from the landscapes to the people, combine in a rich tapestry of lifestyles and culture. Despite its size England has given birth to some of the most renowned world leaders, not only in politics, but in religion, literature, exploration and a host of other areas. It has never given in to the threat of suppression by larger countries, and as such, stands proud in the history books as one of the most impressive and distinguished nations in the world.

CATHEDRALS & ABBEYS

From the earliest Norman churches to modern restorations, England has an abundance of exquisite religious buildings. Every magnificent structure tells its own tale of the country's religious history, its times of upheaval and of prosperity.

Canterbury Cathedral
CANTERBURY KENT

Of all the cowards who eat my bread, are there none to rid me of this turbulent priest?

Henry II had been friends with Thomas Becket for many years and appointed him Archbishop of Canterbury in 1162. It was a tactical move, intended to assert the power of the monarchy over the church, but Becket's diligence and honour meant that Henry did not gain the control he desired, and eventually Becket was forced into exile. On his return six years later his popularity and the support of the Pope forced him to be reinstated to his position. When in anger and frustration Henry spoke these infamous words, little did he imagine the dramatic consequences. Four of his knights, considering it their duty to perform the will of the king, rode to Canterbury where Becket sought sanctuary in the cathedral. Here they struck him dead. Following the king's humiliating penance, which included a barefoot pilgrimage, Becket was canonised.

This tale is the main – and rather macabre – attraction to Canterbury, the main seat of the church of England, but it has many other features worthy of note, including its long history dating back to AD 602, and the tombs of other great historical figures such as Henry IV and Edward, the Black Prince.

Lincoln Cathedral
LINCOLN LINCOLNSHIRE

It was the Celts who first built a small settlement here, called *Lindon* 'hillfort by the lake', and this was expanded by the Romans to become one of the main capitals of Roman Britain. Little evidence remains today of Lincoln's Roman occupation as most buildings were destroyed and rebuilt in medieval times.

The cathedral was begun under the orders of William the Conqueror in 1072, and it took over two decades to complete. Nearly a century after its consecration, however, an earthquake damaged much of the Norman structure, and the present building reveals evidence of a later phase of building dating from the thirteenth century. At this time some parts of the cathedral were repaired and new ones added.

Lincoln's cathedral is a truly extraordinary building, intricately carved with biblical scenes and figures, and with three soaring towers that dominate the town's skyline. Inside, it is no less spectacular, with pleasing irregularities creating an individual atmosphere, and the juxtaposition of the warm golden limestone and the hard, dark marble that characterises many of its assets is both striking and graceful. Perhaps its best-known feature, however, is the Angel Choir – once a popular place for pilgrimages to St Hugh – decorated with thirty elegantly carved angels.

York Minster
YORK NORTH YORKSHIRE

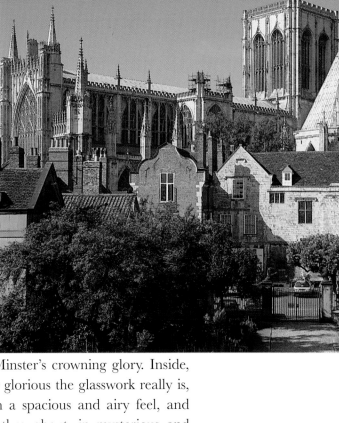

Standing proudly in the north part of the city of York, on the site of an ancient Roman temple dedicated to the goddess Diana, the Minster is the most famous landmark in the county. It is a reflection of the times when York was second only to Canterbury in religious affairs, and is the largest surviving cathedral from medieval times. The site has an earlier association with Christianity: in one of the previous buildings that stood here, King Edwin was converted in AD 627.

The Minster is a toweringly impressive cathedral, encompassing a magnificent blend of architectural styles. Its most impressive feature is the western façade, which boasts a beautifully carved archway and just one of the many windows that are the Minster's crowning glory. Inside, one can see more clearly just how glorious the glasswork really is, endowing the whole interior with a spacious and airy feel, and casting rays of light and colour throughout, in mysterious and spiritual shapes and patterns. This sense of space is also developed by the unusual height and length of the nave, designed in the Decorated style.

Dorchester Abbey
DORCHESTER-ON-THAMES OXFORDSHIRE

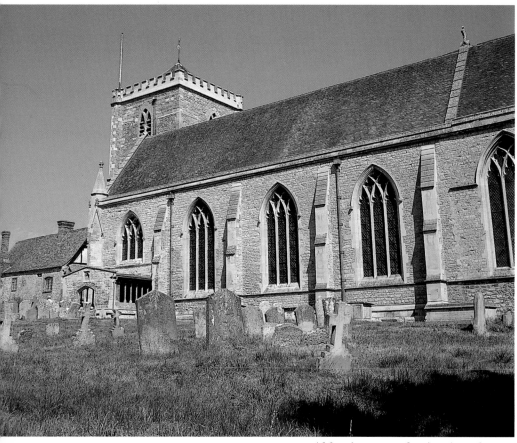

Dorchester began its life as a military settlement in Roman times, and was adopted and expanded by the Saxons to create a thriving town. Today it is a village dominated by picturesque houses, revealing little of its past.

The site of today's Abbey was once a great monastic settlement for the Augustinian order, established in 1140, but most of the domestic buildings were destroyed during the Reformation. Only the present Abbey Church survived the decimation and remained to serve as the parish church. It is likely that the construction of this building was begun before the other buildings that have stood on the site, and is thought to have been completed around 1180. The lovely nave and the choir inside the church date from this Norman period. The Abbey's most fascinating features, however, are the three great windows in the eastern wall of the building. These are actually decorated with biblical scenes, including the sculpted figures of the Twelve Apostles. Additional features were built on to the church over the centuries, including the low tower at the west end, which dates from the seventeenth century.

Winchester Cathedral
WINCHESTER HAMPSHIRE

Winchester Cathedral is the last resting place of many famous figures from English history, and as such is second only to St Paul's Cathedral and Westminster Abbey in London in importance. Its long and illustrious past is evident in the style of the architecture and the atmosphere that permeates this lovely old building.

The first cathedral erected on this site was a Saxon building dedicated to St Swithin – whose remains are interred in the crypt – but there has been a church here since Roman times. Nothing of the Saxon cathedral now remains, however, and the present building is a marvellous combination of styles, due to its lengthy construction, which began in the Early Norman period and lasted for over three hundred years. Among those buried here, is the famed eighteenth-century novelist Jane Austen, her grave slab bearing a simple dedication and conspicuously lacking any reference to her literary works.

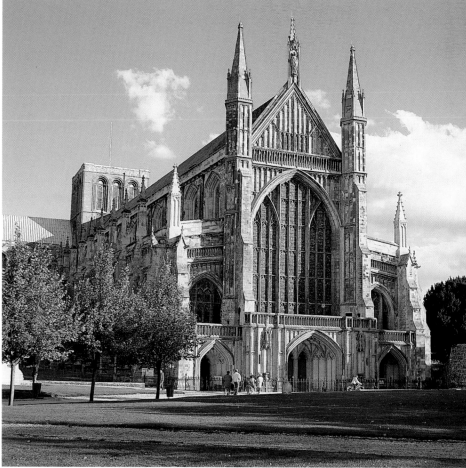

Winchester also has many associations with the Arthurian legends, as early records linked the city with the kingdom of Camelot. The famous Round Table can be found here, giving the names of the knights who belonged to this group. Although it is not the actual table of the legends, but a replica made several centuries after the death of Arthur, it is still a fascinating and haunting historical object.

St Paul's Cathedral
THE CITY LONDON

When the Great Fire of London ravaged the city in 1666 it left a trail of destruction in its wake. Some of the finest buildings in the country were damaged beyond repair. One of these was the cathedral that had stood on the site of the present St Paul's since medieval times. The architect Christopher Wren was commissioned to design a replacement for the cathedral, but his original plans were rejected as being too radical and a more classical compromise was reached. While the ground plan is like that of a medieval church, arranged in the shape of a cross, other elements of the interior reflect Wren's more ambitious Baroque ideas.

Work began on the building in 1675, and was completed in 1710, with the addition of the incredible Dome. St Paul's is the ultimate testimony to Wren's genius, and his tomb in the cathedral bears the inscription 'if you seek his memorial, look around you'. The cathedral contains the tomb of Admiral, Lord Nelson and many other figures who have made their mark on England's history. Today, visitors come in droves to climb the Dome into the spectacular Whispering Gallery, and to admire this magnificent place, which still hosts some of the nation's most important religious events.

Bath Abbey
BATH AVON

In AD 676 a nunnery was built on the site of the present Bath Abbey. This was later converted into a Benedictine Monastery by King Edgar and, in turn, was replaced by a Norman church – eventually left to decay after the bishopric of the area moved to Wells. The Abbey that stands here today was begun in 1499, and its plans incorporated some of the remains of the Norman church.

The exquisite carvings on the façade of Bath Abbey tell the tale of its conception: the Bishop Oliver King had a dream in which he saw multitudes of angels ascending and descending a ladder that led to heaven, and heard voices that he interpreted as instructing him to take the ruined building and create from it a new and impressive place of worship. The carvings depict his vision of the angels, and his own symbol is marked here in the form of an olive tree and a crown.

Work on the Abbey was hindered by the Dissolution, and it was not until 1616 that the Abbey was finally consecrated in all its glory. Its impressive, elaborate exterior is rivalled in magnificence by the interior, which has a host of superb features including nineteenth-century fan vaulting and numerous tombs and memorials.

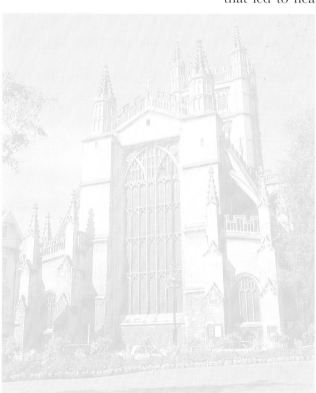

Wells Cathedral
WELLS SOMERSET

The most magnificent of the many medieval structures this beautiful market town boasts is its extraordinary cathedral. Standing on the site of an ancient monastic settlement, founded by the king of Wessex, the present cathedral building dates from 1180, although work continued on it, adding to and enhancing its fine features for many years after this.

Of the exterior of the building, it is the west side that draws the most attention. This fantastic façade was once adorned with over 400 carved figures and statues, which would once have been painted and gilded to make an unforgettable impact on anyone who saw it. These figures were intended to represent the communities of the church and state and, although they have lost their colourful glory and many have been weathered and damaged beyond recognition, a large number still remain in their impressive splendour.

Inside, the genius for carving is further illustrated by a series of fascinating figures in the transept, narrating moral stories including one of a man caught stealing from an orchard. The other attraction inside Wells Cathedral is the well-known astronomical clock, dating from the end of the fourteenth century, which reveals a delightful spectacle of moving knights on chargers as the clock strikes the hour.

Bolton Priory
BOLTON ABBEY NORTH YORKSHIRE

Bolton Priory is considered by many to be the most lovely of all the ruins in England. Despite its fragmented state, the priory still maintains a sense of grandeur that many – more intact – churches lack. The original Augustinian priory was based a few miles away at Embsay, but was moved to Bolton Abbey in the middle of the twelfth century by Lady Alice de Romille, to commemorate the drowning of her son in the River Strid. Like most other settlements, the priory suffered in the Dissolution, when only the nave, which was also used as a parish church, was spared the destruction.

Situated a short walk from the confusingly-named village of Bolton Abbey, the priory stands surveying a landscape of verdant meadows, streams and woodland. The graceful scenery has inspired artists, poets and writers to immortalise it in their works. It is a haunting place, characterised by small pathways overgrown with grass and wild flowers. The surrounding area has some magnificent walks, particularly through to Bolton Hall, the ancestral home of the Dukes of Devonshire.

Norwich Cathedral
NORWICH NORFOLK

The spire of this beautiful cathedral soars up to a height of 96 metres, dominating the skyline for miles around – the second highest church spire in the country after that of Salisbury cathedral. It owes its brilliant aspect to careful preservation of the startling white stone used in its construction, this lends it an air of majesty to equal any other structure in England.

A Norman building, Norwich cathedral was begun in 1096 by the then-bishop Herbert de Losinga, but the work was not completed until after his death. Typically, elements have been added throughout the centuries. The spire that tops the building today is not the original, which collapsed in the fourteenth century. It was replaced by the present one, which exhibits the rise of the Decorated style in architecture. The magnificent Perpendicular window that is the glory of the western façade was created in the fifteenth century when the building was undergoing some restoration to the nave. Inside the cathedral the feeling of light and space is enhanced by pale brickwork and large windows.

Coventry Cathedral
COVENTRY WEST MIDLANDS

The city of Coventry is dominated by the imposing shape of its cathedral. A large part of the present building dates from the 1950s – it was rebuilt after a devastating air raid during the Second World War left it, and many other buildings in the city, in ruins. Hidden within the modern architecture, however, traces of its past can be found, most notably the tall steeple that still towers above the cathedral and dates from early in the twentieth century. A canopied path leads from the new cathedral to the fragments of the old one.

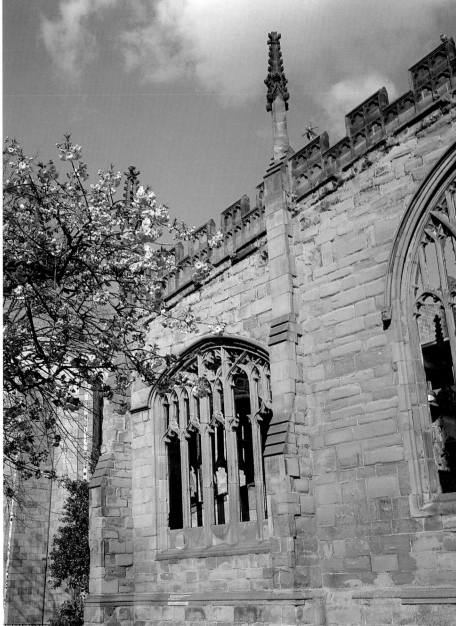

The new St Michael's Cathedral was designed by Sir Basil Spence, and, as is typical of much twentieth-century architecture, has been the subject of some controversy over the years. Constructed of pink sandstone, the cathedral has an unusual but lovely aspect, and its feeling of lightness and elegance is reflected in the interior. The predominance of stained glass is overwhelming, with huge panels stretching to the ceiling, allowing light to flood the cathedral. In its modernity, Coventry Cathedral is a splendid place of worship, and the relics of the old church, now a memorial shrine to the war dead are an evocative testimony to the country's more recent past.

Hereford Cathedral
HEREFORD HEREFORD & WORCESTER

The cathedral at Hereford is dedicated to St Ethelbert who is buried here. History relates that Ethelbert, the king of East Anglia, wanted to marry the daughter of King Offa of Mercia, and visited him at his court. For reasons that remain unexplained, Offa took it upon himself to cut off Ethelbert's head. On the day of the burial, it is said that a column of light shone down from the heavens, and a few days later, a local nobleman dreamed that Ethelbert was unhappy with his burial place. So, exhuming both body and head, he travelled – following another guiding light – until he reached Hereford, and there he re-buried the saint.

In the eighteenth century, the early Norman tower crumbled under its own weight, taking with it large parts of the nave. Although most of the building is made from sandstone, including the fourteenth-century tower that still stands, opposing views on how it should be restored have resulted in a strange mixture of architectural styles, which, although fascinating, has destroyed the pleasing aesthetic harmony that would once have characterised it. The cathedral's most treasured possession is the famous *Mappa Mundi*: Richard Haldingham's huge map of the world dating from 1275.

Tewkesbury Abbey
TEWKESBURY GLOUCESTERSHIRE

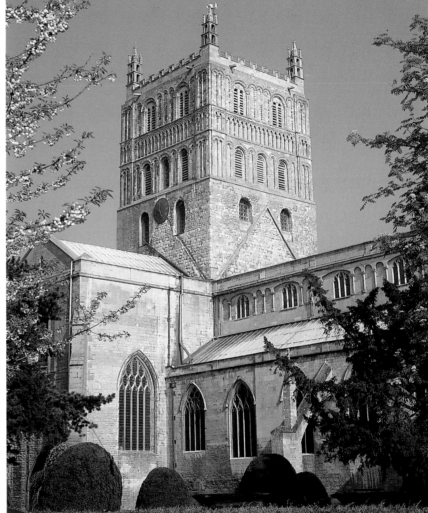

Tewkesbury is perhaps most famous for being the site of the last great battle in the Wars of the Roses. It was here that the Yorkists, after a long struggle, finally defeated the Lancastrians in 1472. After the battle, the abbey at Tewkesbury was re-consecrated, and the building that stands there today remains almost as it was all those centuries ago.

Norman in style, the abbey was begun in 1092, and the final part – the enormous central tower which is the largest in the world – was completed in 1160. Inside the abbey, fourteen huge pillars in the nave soar to the ceiling, reflecting the sheer scale and grandeur of the building, inside and out. Carvings on the tower vaulting show circles of suns depicting the victory of the Yorkists in the nearby Bloody Meadow, and a pavement plaque commemorates the young Prince Edward who died in the battle. Everywhere, there are reminders of the city's most illustrious historical event.

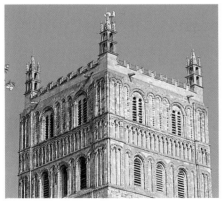

The Abbey has been extended over the years, particularly in the fourteenth century, but the most splendid additions are the wonderful Perpendicular windows that date from the seventeenth century. Despite its monastic associations, the Abbey survived the Dissolution, although most of the surrounding buildings were completely destroyed.

Durham Cathedral
DURHAM COUNTY DURHAM

The massive cathedral at Durham is one of the finest examples of Norman architecture left in England. Built in 1133, it has survived remarkably well, although parts of the interior were destroyed in 1650 by Cromwell's prisoners, who were kept here.

The most outstanding part of the building must surely be the nave. It exhibits a revolutionary structure, using pointed arches supported by immense stone pillars to give an incredibly high ceiling. It was the first time this design was used in a cathedral and the result is an overwhelming sense of space and grandeur. Amongst those interred here are the Venerable Bede and St Cuthbert.

In the Middle Ages Durham Cathedral drew many fugitives who sought sanctuary within its hallowed walls. The north-west door of the building has a knocker in the shape of a grotesque head, dating from the twelfth century, which was used to alert the monks to their presence. There was also a small room with a window overlooking this entrance, where the monks would keep a look-out for those in need – and for any danger that might have followed them.

Whitby Abbey
WHITBY NORTH YORKSHIRE

The fragments that remain of the once-illustrious Whitby Abbey stand on the site of an ancient monastic community founded in AD 657 by St Hilda of Hartlepool. For three hundred years the settlement prospered, becoming one of the main centres of Christianity in England. Its importance can be gauged by the fact that in AD 664, it was host to the famous Synod of Whitby, a meeting at which church leaders gathered to decide on which should be the ruling religion in England – Roman Catholicism or Celtic Christianity. The ruins of the Abbey that can be seen today date from the beginning of the thirteenth century, and although large parts have now been completely destroyed, enough remains for the visitor to appreciate the great beauty of the original building.

The Abbey is situated at the top of a steep cliff and the views that surround this area, particularly out across the sea are truly breathtaking. One of the most unusual features here is the series of pirate gravestones that can be found by the path leading up to the Abbey. These recumbent stones lie in the grass and are marked with no Christian symbols, only a skull and crossbones. In combination with the eerie ruins of the Abbey they hold a mysterious and fascinating appeal.

LANDSCAPES & SEASCAPES

Both inland and along the coastline, England exhibits some breathtaking and diverse scenery. Undulating hills and deep valleys are contrasted with rocky cliffs and the rolling ocean waves.

Bedruthan Steps
NEAR NEWQUAY CORNWALL

This part of Cornwall is renowned for its fantastic rocky scenery, and the Bedruthan Steps are just a few of the dramatic slate outcrops, harsh cliffs and broken rocks that characterise this area. They are situated not far from the busy fishing port of Newquay, one of England's most popular holiday destinations, with some of the country's finest strips of beach.

Bedruthan is a nature reserve situated along a coastal walk, and is typified by these large, erratic rocks scattered around the clifftop. Legend has it that they are stepping stones made by a giant named Bedruthan, but this is a nineteenth-century tale, and the rocks have evidently been here for many ages before then.

The landscapes here are at their most breathtaking during the winter, when stormy skies and high winds lend a mysterious and foreboding aspect to the scene, with the wild waves breaking noisily below. At such times, the Steps are a dangerous place to be, as the rock can be unstable in parts, particularly along the coastal path. On calm days like this, however, the blue of the sea complements the grey rocks and green countryside, providing a pleasant and inviting spectacle.

The Chiltern Hills
TURVILLE BUCKINGHAMSHIRE

Stretching through Oxfordshire, Buckinghamshire and Hertfordshire, the Chiltern Hills contain some of the most unspoilt and lovely areas in the country. The scenery changes throughout the long stretch of the hills, and includes picturesque villages, dense woodland, and rolling grassy hills.

The chalk land of the Chilterns was once a cold and desolate place, a natural landmark that divided London and the north-west of England, making communication between two parts of the country nearly impossible. Ancient roads follow the line of the valley through which the hills traverse, and the large expanses of wood and forest that are scattered around the Chilterns once hid bandits and highwaymen. There is a timeless quality to these remote areas that is both mysterious and exciting.

The Hills offer some of the best walking areas in the south of England, particularly along the famous Ridgeway Route, with magnificent vistas of the surrounding counties and a few archaeological relics of ancient times to stumble across, including chalk crosses carved into the hillsides. The mesmerising greenery of the hills, the hidden villages, the beautiful downs and the rich valleys combine to make up a spectacular landscape.

Ilfracombe Harbour
ILFRACOMBE DEVON

Ilfracombe is marked by its spectacularly dramatic cliff scenery and its lovely beach front, which has become the most popular resort in the north of Devon. It has retained an atmosphere of undisturbed beauty, unlike most other seaside resorts in England, as any extensive development is prevented by the impressive cliffs that surround the beach front and harbour.

The town and harbour have remained pretty much the same as they were in the days when Ilfracombe rose to prosperity in Edwardian times. It was then that many of the English seaside resorts became fashionable as summer residences for the upper classes, who would escape from the big cities to take in the healthy sea air.

Inland, the landscape around Ilfracombe is just as beautiful as the beach scenery. Woodland and fields lie scattered between the rocks, the grassy land stretching out to the cliff edges.

Beachy Head
EASTBOURNE EAST SUSSEX

The breathtaking headland of Beachy Head is made up of towering chalk cliffs, dropping a sheer 160 metres into the sea. The headland forms just part of a series of dramatic cliffs along the South Downs. Its name comes from the French *beau chef* meaning 'beautiful head', a truly appropriate description of this exceptional part of Sussex.

Below the cliff, standing in isolated splendour, is the lighthouse. This was built in 1902 to replace the old Belle Tout Lighthouse that had stood here since the 1830s to warn sailors of the dangers that lurked in the mists. The sea here is unbroken by beach, crashing violently against the bottom of the cliffs.

Nestling under the protection of the headland lies the town of Eastbourne, once a group of small villages that expanded until they eventually formed a town. Like many of England's seaside resorts, Eastbourne first achieved popularity in Victorian times, and has maintained this favour largely due to the fact that commercial development is not allowed along the seafront, thus ensuring the town has escaped the rising tide of resort entertainments that characterise many other seaside towns.

Rugged Coastline
TINTAGEL CORNWALL

The name Tintagel conjures up magical images of King Arthur and his Knights of the Round Table, and the air of mystery that surrounds the name is reflected in the wild and intriguing scenery that characterises this part of Cornwall. The coastline is wild and unspoilt and offers a vista of harsh crags weathered by the strong gales and storms that roll in from the Atlantic. The rocks and crags in this area have proved to be extremely dangerous, and the waves that crash below the looming headland of Tintagel Head conceal the wrecks of numerous ships.

The formidable ruins of Tintagel Castle add to the untamed atmosphere pervading the area, and this ancient air encourages the tales of Arthurian association, despite the fact that the castle is really a stronghold dating only as far back as Norman times. The legends themselves go back further, and it was the twelfth-century historian Geoffrey of Monmouth who first suggested that Tintagel was the place where King Arthur was born. It is an association of which the town is proud, and all over the area, tales of Arthur, Uther Pendragon, Tristan and Iseult and many other figures are commemorated and perpetuated.

Matlock Bath
MATLOCK DERBYSHIRE

Matlock is actually divided into a number of separate areas, including Matlock Bridge and Matlock Bank. Matlock Bath is a small but picturesque village in the heart of Derbyshire's Peak District. Lying near the Derwent, it is protected by the limestone gorge created by the river. This craggy and dramatic scenery provides a daunting but fascinating backdrop to the village.

On the opposite bank of the river from Matlock Bath, the impressive High Tor rears up, the most fantastic natural feature in this part of the ravine. High Tor is a limestone crag that juts out across the valley, at a height over 120 metres above the river. The dramatic scenery was part of the attraction when the village rose to prosperity in the mid-1800s. Here, amidst the rolling hills and limestone ravines, natural springs rich in minerals well up from the earth. It was this important natural feature that drew crowds to Matlock, swelling it into a small but influential spa town. A local citizen, John Smedley, opened the first hydropathic centre here in 1853, and from that time, it drew crowds of people coming to take the waters. It has ceased to serve this purpose, but its magnificent setting and historic past ensure its popularity with visitors to the Peak District.

Cheddar Gorge
CHEDDAR SOMERSET

This part of Somerset is characterised by its dramatic rock scenery, and the most famous feature of this landscape is Cheddar Gorge. A narrow path cuts its way through the limestone cliffs that tower on either side of it. The path winds for approximately two miles and, gouged into the ravine walls, are myriad caves and crevices. These caves form some of the most fascinating natural landmarks in the country; an eerie collection of dark caverns, filled with amazing stalactites and strange formations weathered out of the limestone rocks. The caves have an air of ancient secrecy about them, inhabited as they were by people from Stone Age times.

The town of Cheddar, famed for its cheese, lies at the mouth of the gorge at the foot of the Mendip Hills. The rolling landscape of the plateau gives little indication of the complexity of caves and passages that run beneath it. Only occasionally, where it is broken by the sheer grey gorges, does one realise that there is more to this part of the country than immediately meets the eye.

Bournemouth Beach
BOURNEMOUTH DORSET

Bournemouth is a relatively modern resort compared with some of its neighbouring beaches. It grew up in the early 1800s when a local Lord named Louis Tregonwell decided to construct a summer home here. At that time, the area was characterised by beautiful untamed moorland, broken by the rough cliffs and the inland ravines that can still be seen today. The captivating surroundings soon proved a popular attraction, and more and more wealthy people moved their summer residences to this stretch of the coast, until eventually the town expanded, and the seafront became a bustling resort.

Inland, the scenery is dominated by pine trees, the first of which were planted by Tregonwell when he originally moved here. These pine woods have grown and spread and are now a major – and unusual – part of the countryside. The sandy strip of beach has retained its popularity since it first became fashionable in Victorian times, mainly due to its sheltered situation at the foot of the cliffs, and the temperate climate that is typical of much of the southern coastal region of England.

Drystone Wall
UPPER SLAUGHTER GLOUCESTERSHIRE

Much of the Cotswold landscape is divided into neat fields like this by drystone walls. The presence of numerous rocks in this area has been exploited since the Iron Age, when settlers realised the potential of a landscape covered with rocky promontories, ideal for setting up forts and other defences against attack. The abundance of stone for building materials was simply an added advantage. The remains of many of these Iron Age constructions, and those of later inhabitants, can still be seen in the grassy slopes of the Cotswold Hills.

The rock is still a major source of the area's affluence today. Because of its unusual properties, the stone is relatively soft when it is first quarried, but it hardens on exposure to the air, to create sturdy blocks that are ideal for building. A further property of this useful material is that, once hardened, it can be easily split, and a flourishing trade in roofing tiles and slates has resulted. Examples of this stone can be seen all over the Cotswold countryside, and the houses – ranging from a beautiful golden honey colour to the lightest slate grey – have become a characteristic feature of the landscape.

Great Yarmouth Seafront
GREAT YARMOUTH NORFOLK

Great Yarmouth has a reputation for being a popular, crowded resort dominated by the usual seafront entertainments, but it is also an area with a long and illustrious history. The town itself began to prosper in the thirteenth century, when the city walls were first constructed, and despite the damage done by both time and the Second World War, some buildings and parts of the original city wall remain in all their medieval splendour.

The town owes its prosperity to its North Sea

location. Lying on the Yare peninsula where the river meets with the Waveney and the Bure to flow into the sea, Great Yarmouth has naturally turned to the ocean as its source of industry and commerce. In past centuries, the people of Yarmouth have made their livings fishing for herring, whaling and even looting the wrecks of ships that foundered off its coastline. In the past the port was put to use as a shipyard and point for the oil and gas rigs offshore, and it remains an important asset to the town, providing a direct route to a number of European countries.

Sheep Grazing
WHARFEDALE NORTH YORKSHIRE

Epitomised by traditional Dales villages and gentle, undulating hills, Wharfedale is a picture-postcard part of the country. It is the southernmost valley of the Dales, and reaches out to the east in a wide and dramatic sweep. The River Wharfe flows from the city of Leeds through numerous villages and small towns, and past many haunting but fascinating ruins, such as Bolton Priory, that lie scattered around the countryside.

The central town in the area is Grassington, a small but lively town with steep cobbled streets and marvellous views, but the path of the valley encompasses many smaller villages such as Burnsall, equally idyllic in aspect. Farmland predominates here, and much of the landscape consists of verdant fields, where cows and sheep graze peacefully, and old stone farmhouses stand in graceful situations. Each part of Wharfedale seems to have its own individual character and atmosphere: sometimes, the Wharfe flows quietly through acres of silent countryside, in other places it gushes down falls and under bridges, rivalling the bustle of the nearby towns. Wherever one travels in the valley, it is impossible to escape the richness and majesty of this beautiful area.

Dartmoor Ponies
DARTMOOR DEVON

The rough, daunting landscape of Dartmoor stretches through a large part of Devon. It is a diverse and wildly beautiful part of the West Country, characterised in some parts by exposed granite rocks, in others by marshy bog land and vast expanses of heather. The most distinctive parts of Dartmoor are its famous Tors, massive grey hills of granite that have been worn by time and the elements to create a series of mysterious and impressive monuments.

Dartmoor was once home to Bronze and Stone Age peoples, who were drawn by the large amounts of building stone and the abundance of water available. Today, remnants of these ancient races survive in the form of ruined huts, stone circles and primitive roadways. Dartmoor is now uninhabited by humans, and the only signs of life are the semi-wild ponies that roam the moors grazing on the flat lowland plains. Although these ponies can be seen on the moors in all weathers, they are not completely wild, and most of them belong to local farmers. Today, they are left in peace, but in previous centuries they were used to carry the copper, lead and tin, from the mines that were scattered around the moor.

Derwent Water
KESWICK CUMBRIA

Despite being one of the most popular of the Cumbrian Lakes, Derwent Water manages to maintain its atmosphere of peace and tranquillity, and its own individual character. The awe-inspiring beauty of the lake is enhanced by its magnificent setting; caught between the domineering mountains of Skiddaw and Scarfell, its scenery is typified by rolling hills and woodland, and miles of undisturbed pathways offering walks with views of unsurpassed grandeur.

Derwent Water is a placid area stretching three miles in length and only one mile in width. The most enchanting features of the lake, however, are the small islands that lie scattered throughout the water. The main one, Derwent Island, was actually inhabited in the sixteenth century. The atmosphere of the lake and its surroundings changes dramatically throughout the seasons, and according to the weather: a bright, shimmering place one minute, and hung with a mysterious foreboding the next. This atmosphere is enhanced by the gentle shifts of the water as the River Derwent flows through the lake. Derwent Water is also a paradise for anglers, who come to sit peacefully along its banks, fishing for the salmon and trout that inhabit this majestic lake.

Seascape
LAND'S END CORNWALL

The Scilly Isles represent the extreme south-western region of England, but on the mainland, it is Land's End that marks this point. This impressive headland is the final section of a long stretch of rocky granite landscapes that begin on Dartmoor to the east. Made up of harsh grey rocks, the peninsula is a wild and magnificent place, with pounding waves crashing against the cliffs, which rise in a sheer 60-metre wall.

From this vantage point, it is possible to look out across the Atlantic. On a clear day, the Scilly Isles are visible, and over a mile out to sea stands the Longships lighthouse. By far the most dramatic features to be seen from here, however, are the fantastic outcrops along the cliffside. They have all been christened with romantic names – the Irish Lady and the Armed Knight among them – to describe the strange shapes that have been formed from the granite by centuries of erosion.

The area around Land's End is also known for its many ancient monuments: standing stones and cairns lie scattered around the countryside, providing a fascinating diversion for those who come to admire the breathtaking views, and adding to the timeless and elemental atmosphere that pervades the peninsula.

ARCHITECTURE

Throughout England, fine examples of architecture can be seen from all periods in the country's rich history. Houses, palaces, bridges and public buildings stand in a graceful testimony to the ingenuity and imagination of their designers.

Tower Bridge
THE CITY LONDON

Lying proudly under the protection of the foreboding Tower of London, Tower Bridge is a fine construction made up of a long walkway across the river, marked by two immense towers at either end. Its size and distinctive design have made it another well-known symbol of the city of London since it opened in 1894.

Built to span the Thames here, the bridge had to be designed in such a way that water vessels could still travel up the river without hindrance. To facilitate this, the bridge is made up of two drawbridges, which are raised to allow ships to pass underneath. The sight of the drawbridges being pulled up is a popular one, drawing crowds of visitors every day to catch the bridge at half-mast.

The pulley system for the drawbridges was operated by steam engines when the bridge was first built, and it was not until 1976 that these were finally abandoned in favour of a more efficient electrical system. The large old engines are now displayed in a fascinating exhibition about this intriguing landmark, in the museum that is housed in the south tower of the bridge.

River Severn Road Bridge
BRISTOL AVON

Officially opened by the present Queen in 1966, this is the first of two road bridges that span the River Severn across to Wales on the opposite bank. At the time of its construction it ranked amongst the longest bridges in the world, although this position has long since been usurped. The bridge was much needed to serve this stretch of the river, where there was no means of access into Wales. The nearest alternative route was via a bridge sixty miles away at Gloucester. Designed by Freeman Fox, a firm of consulting engineers, the Severn Bridge was the first bridge in the world to employ incline suspension cables. These were an innovative idea that provided a more stable deck and increased protection from the high winds that could whistle through the river valley. Despite this, the bridge is still forced to close in high winds. While the structure itself is safe, its design leaves the traffic crossing the bridge dangerously exposed to these winds.

The second road bridge is a more recent structure and was opened in 1996. Situated three miles downstream from the first, its designers took advantage of the advances in civil engineering, and included windshields to provide a stable passageway for road traffic across the Severn.

Royal Crescent
BATH AVON

The Royal Crescent in Bath is a perfect example of the Palladian style of architecture that took the country by storm during the eighteenth century. Bath, particularly, contains some of the finest architecture to be found anywhere in England.

Royal Crescent is a magnificent sweep of thirty houses built in an arched street. The houses were designed by the second John Wood and date from 1767. Wood's intention was to break away from the typical town square style that had characterised city residences for many years, thereby creating a new type of city architecture. Each of these terraced houses is exactly the same, and together they form a grand and majestic façade, enhanced by the golden glow of their brickwork. In front of the Crescent lies a beautiful lawn, and the houses command a perfect view of the surrounding countryside.

Number 1 Royal Crescent has become a popular attraction in Bath, as much of the interior has been recreated to illustrate its original appearance. The rooms contain an impressive variety of genuine nineteenth-century furniture and fittings, making it possible to glimpse how residents of this glorious street would once have lived.

Tyne Bridge
NEWCASTLE-UPON-TYNE   TYNE & WEAR

Six bridges span the River Tyne in this area, including the famous road-and-rail bridge designed by Robert Stevenson in the 1840s. It is the Tyne Bridge, however, that is most commonly associated with Newcastle-upon-Tyne, and which has now become a symbol of this thriving industrial city, and an integral part of its unique and lively character.

Construction began on the Tyne Bridge in 1925, and it was to mark the beginning of a new and radical phase in bridge design and construction. By the time it was officially opened by George V in 1928, the Tyne Bridge boasted the largest arch of its kind in the world. This was a great achievement, but unfortunately, it was a record the Tyne Bridge was not to hold for long. The design proved to be the inspiration for a new bridge being built on the opposite side of the world – in Sydney Harbour – which took the record on its completion, just a few months after the Tyne Bridge was opened. Despite this, Newcastle's bridge has remained one of the North's most famous landmarks, and is acknowledged as a magnificent feat of engineering.

Pulteney Bridge
BATH AVON

The River Avon lends much charm to the city of Bath – a magnificent city, alive with history and marvellous architecture. Over the centuries, many local figures have designed developments to improve and enhance the city. One of these figures was Sir William Pulteney, who decided to build an area on the east bank of the Avon, which would be the epicentre of upper-class living, dominated by grand residences along carefully arranged streets, avenues and parks.

Pulteney Bridge was constructed as a link from this development on the east side to the city centre on the west. Pulteney commissioned a young Scottish architect called Robert Adam to create his bridge. Adam came up with an elegant design, based on an Italianate structure, incorporating three picturesque arches. It was completed in the 1770s, but Pulteney's dream was never to be fulfilled completely. His plans for the residential area were thwarted by financial difficulties, and today the streets reflect little of Sir William's original vision. The bridge today is lined with shops that still attract people to this lovely landmark.

The Radcliffe Camera
OXFORD OXFORDSHIRE

This unusual piece of architecture lords over its own square – Radcliffe Square – complete with pavements and lawns. Its somewhat isolated situation only serves to enhance its dramatic effect. The Camera was built during the first half of the eighteenth century and took over ten years to construct. It was the brainchild of architect James Gibbs, who had been commissioned to design a building in which to house the science library belonging to Dr John Radcliffe.

Radcliffe was one of Oxford's most eminent citizens, and his name can be found all over the city, most notably in the Oxford Infirmary and the Observatory, which he also helped to fund. In his will, he bequeathed a large sum of money in order that a library could be built for his books.

The Radcliffe Camera is Baroque in style, with a remarkable octagonal base, and topped by a marvellous dome. It is one of the best examples of its kind left in England. Today, it is still used for its original purpose, as part of the world-famous Bodleian Library.

Bridge of Sighs
CAMBRIDGE CAMBRIDGESHIRE

The Bridge of Sighs in Cambridge is just one of a number that bear this name. Like these, its construction is based on the original Bridge of Sighs in Venice, so called because at one time it stretched from part of a prison, across the river to the place of execution. Although the title is less than appropriate for many of its English counterparts, the romance of the name seems to suit the charm and tranquillity of its situation in Cambridge.

Hidden away behind the impressive buildings of St John's College, the mock-Gothic arched Bridge of Sighs spans the River Cam from the Chapel Court to the

New Court. It is one of two bridges that cross the Cam here. The other – the Old Bridge – is a marvellous structure by Robert Grumbold which dates from the turn of the eighteenth century. The Bridge of Sighs is a picturesque complement to the older bridge. It was built in 1831 to designs by Henry Hutchinson, with the intention of allowing access from the old college to the New Court across the river, while remaining on college grounds. Although the public are not allowed to use the bridge, it can be appreciated from the comfort of one of the punts that travel leisurely down the River Cam along this stretch.

Royal Pavilion
BRIGHTON EAST SUSSEX

An appropriate reflection of the extravagant tastes of its founder, George III, the Royal Pavilion lies in the middle of the Old Steine in the heart of Brighton, a lavish, exotic and somewhat unexpected relic of the Regency period.

The old farmhouse that once stood on this spot was replaced by a grand villa, its style mainly Palladian, with a few oriental influences. But this was not enough for the prince, who ordered an even more ornate palace to be built as his seaside residence. The famous architect John Nash received this commission and concocted the unprecedented mixture of architectural styles that make up the Pavilion as it stands today. Drawing from Chinese, Indian and Gothic influences, Nash created an impressive building with domes and pinnacles, balconies and carvings with an unusual iron framework.

George III spent many splendid weeks here until his death, when Queen Victoria's very different tastes led her to move the royal seaside residence to the Isle of Wight, and removed all items of value from the Pavilion to Buckingham Palace. Today, many of these have been returned to Brighton, and the Pavilion has been restored to resemble fairly closely the way it was in its Regency heyday.

Magdalen Bridge
OXFORD OXFORDSHIRE

Magdalen College is set in the finest of all the grounds scattered throughout Oxford. The college itself was founded in the middle of the fifteenth century by William of Waynfleete, who was then Bishop of Winchester, and the buildings that remain from this time are magnificent examples of medieval architecture. These include the large tower that dominates the college site.

The college grounds are unique in having their own deer park, and this extensive area of land stretches through a number of other beautiful walks including water meadows, which provide some unusual flora and fauna for this part of the country. Addison's Walk, one of these meadows, stretches down to the River Cherwell and Magdalen Bridge. This charming structure was designed by John Gwynn and built between 1772 and 1779 to provide access from the Magdalen College side of the Cherwell to the walks on the opposite bank. It was widened in the late nineteenth century to improve this access. Set against the backdrop of the parks and trees, the arched bridge with its gold and grey brickwork makes a picturesque complement to the scenery, and is a popular place for those enjoying the landscape from the punts and rowing boats that are a common sight up and down the Cherwell.

Iron Bridge
RIVER SEVERN SHROPSHIRE

On first impressions, the countryside surrounding the town of Ironbridge reveals little of its great past, but hidden in the hillsides are relics of a great industrial age. The Iron Bridge is the most famous, and the most magnificent, remnant of the area's period of prosperity. Before this was built, the only method of crossing the River Severn here was by boat or via a medieval bridge which lay a few miles away. The idea for a bridge across the river here was first put forward by Abraham Darby III. The proposal was agreed, and plans suggested for how this was to be constructed. The architect Thomas Farnolls Pritchard drew up designs for a bridge made of cast iron – a feat never attempted before. Although the bridge that stands there now does not exactly reflect Pritchard's original plans, it is generally accepted that he was chiefly responsible for the design.

The bridge, a structure that combined beauty with strength through its arched sides and iron railings, was opened in 1781. For the first time, a working model illustrated the newly discovered properties of cast iron. Today it is still an awe-inspiring piece of engineering, and an enduring symbol of the Industrial Revolution in England.

The Houses of Parliament
WESTMINSTER LONDON

Parliament has only been housed in these magnificent buildings since the sixteenth century. For over 500 years prior to this, they were the seat of the English monarchy. The present Parliament buildings – named correctly as the Palace of Westminster – stand on the site of the original royal residence built by Edward the Confessor, a purpose for which it was used until Henry VIII moved the residence to Whitehall.

The House of Commons originally had its home in the chapter house of Westminster Abbey, but after Henry VIII's death, it was moved into St Stephen's Chapel in the old Palace of Westminster. The buildings that lie on the banks of the Thames today, however, are not those of the original Palace, which was gutted by fire in 1834. The architect Charles Barry won the competition to design the new home for Parliament, and the breathtaking, Gothic-style construction that dominates Westminster now stands as a testimony to his genius. The design reflects the Palace's majestic history, with ornate carvings, turrets and three tremendous towers.

Inside, the building is no less impressive, a grand mass of offices and rooms, and, of course, the House of Commons, located at the north end and the House of Lords in the south, where public galleries allow visitors to witness parliamentary debates.

King's College
CAMBRIDGE CAMBRIDGESHIRE

King's College – and all the magnificent buildings it encompasses – is arguably the most beautiful of all the Cambridge colleges. Founded in 1441 by Henry VI, little of the original collection of buildings survives today, but for a few fragments still visible. The most notable of these is the King's College Chapel, certainly the most admired of all Cambridge's buildings, and the object of immense pride.

The Chapel is situated on the north side of the Great Court of the college. It is built of white limestone which lends it a serenely majestic aura, enhanced by the simplicity of the design and the unusual lack of decorative carving that usually adorns the exterior of such constructions. Inside, however, is some of the most marvellous and extravagant decoration in the city, including exotic fan vaulting and the impressive stained glass windows dating from the sixteenth century. Building began on the chapel in 1446, not long after the college itself was founded, but it was added to by both Henry VII and Henry VIII over the next century.

King's College Chapel has earned its fame through song, story and painting, being the subject of works by the artist Turner and the poet Wordsworth to name but two, and the home of a famed choir.

Christ Church College
OXFORD OXFORDSHIRE

Christ Church is the largest of Oxford University's colleges. It was founded as Cardinal's College in 1525 by Wolsey, Henry VIII's infamous advisor. The college was not to enjoy his patronage for very long, though, and after he lost favour with the king, Henry refounded it as King's College; it was later renamed Christ Church.

The most famous and unique feature of the college is the Christ Church itself. Although this still serves as the college chapel, it has also been the city's cathedral since the sixteenth century. The diminutive size of the cathedral – England's smallest – does not detract from its splendour. It is actually older than the college, and was once part of an ancient settlement founded by St Frideswide. Today, most of the construction dates from medieval times, and is a splendid example of Norman architecture. Other elements have been added to the college buildings since this time, most notably the great bell tower, known affectionately as Tom Tower, which was part of plans drawn up for the college by the renowned architect Christopher Wren – who was also responsible for the rebuilding of St Paul's Cathedral in London after the Great Fire of 1666.

Clapper Bridge
EASTLEACH GLOUCESTERSHIRE

Clapper bridges like this one can be seen spanning streams and ditches all over the English countryside. It is one of the earliest forms of bridge structure, and many of them have been in place for centuries. They can most often be seen in areas like Gloucestershire, or the West Country where the abundance of stone made them cheap and easy to construct. They are less common in parts of the country characterised by the chalk or limestone landscapes, where the local materials were not strong enough to build these simple slab bridges.

Many clapper bridges are constructed of one single slab of stone laid across from one bank of the stream to the other, but where the ditch is wider – and if the stream is shallow enough – piles of stones would be laid down across the water and smaller slabs used to connect them. These structures were strong, they needed to be sturdy enough to carry the weight of people and pack animals, and were virtually indestructible, which is why so many of them remain today. They make an enchanting addition to the countryside, often found in some of the most remote and beautiful parts of the country.

Royal Albert Hall
KENSINGTON LONDON

This distinctive red-brick building, which stands opposite Hyde Park in the centre of London, has become the most famous concert hall in the city. It is the most revolutionary of the Victorian constructions in this area, abandoning all the ideas of modest design that usually characterise the architecture of this time. When it was completed in 1871, the Royal Albert Hall was considered to be both daring and magnificent.

The man who designed the building was an engineer called Francis Fowke, who drew his inspiration for the concert hall from the Roman amphitheatres. The financial backing for these ambitious plans came from an unusual source – seats in the yet-to-be-constructed theatre were sold on a leasehold to the wealthy people of the area, and although ownership of these has largely passed back to the Albert Hall, some private ownership of certain seats continues.

Today, the Royal Albert Hall hosts numerous spectacular events, but the most famous and the most popular is the extravagant series of classical concerts known as the 'Proms', which take place here annually, delighting crowds of thousands in the hall, and the many more who watch them on television.

Clifton Suspension Bridge
BRISTOL AVON

When William Vick, a Bristol wine merchant, died in 1754, he left a small bequest and instructions that this money was not to be touched until enough had accumulated to fund a bridge to span the Avon Gorge. It would be 100 years before his vision was realised.

In 1829 the city announced a competition for the design of the planned bridge, and this was won by Isambard Brunel. Brunel's original plans were for a lavish Egyptian-style bridge, complete with towers and sphinxes at either end, but sadly these adornments never made it further than the drawing board. Work on the bridge was slow, hindered by financial and other difficulties, and the architect, like the sponsor, never saw his work completed.

Clifton Suspension Bridge was finally opened in 1864, an incredible, nerve-wracking achievement. It runs for more than 200 metres in length, over the extremely deep Avon Gorge. At night it is lit by thousands of bulbs, making a spectacular and awe-inspiring sight that has justifiably become one of Bristol's most famous landmarks.

LAKES & WATERWAYS

From the natural beauty of the country's plentiful rivers and the magnificence of the Cumbrian Lake District to its industrially significant canals, the waterways of England are an essential and graceful part of the landscape.

Kennet and Avon Canal
LITTLE BEDWYN WILTSHIRE

Forging a path from the Thames at Reading, the Kennet and Avon Canal passes through some marvellous countryside and bustling towns, such as Devizes and Bath, before ending its 100-mile journey at Avonmouth. The canal is still in use both for transportation and pleasure boating. Along its course is a total of 105 locks. Many of these are concentrated in areas where the canal rises to nearly 200 metres above sea level, while flatter terrain goes for long distances without a single lock.

The idea for a canal to connect the two stretches of the Thames and Avon rivers came from Henry Briggs in 1626. The plan was to create a link between these two rivers, providing a waterway that could run from Bristol as far as Reading, greatly improving the commercial prospects of these towns and the areas that lay in between. After nearly 100 years, the first waterway was opened between Reading and Newbury, alerting people to the prospects that could be opened up if this were to be applied to Bath. The entire project was not completed until nearly a century later, but at last the two cities were connected by what is now known as the Kennet and Avon Canal.

Grand Union Canal
SOULBURY BUCKINGHAMSHIRE

Flowing through the counties of Bedfordshire, Buckinghamshire and Northamptonshire before branching off to the North, the Grand Union Canal is an amalgamation of eight waterways, most of which were constructed when these controlled passages of water were the height of fashion in the eighteenth century. The largest water passage was the Grand Junction Canal, built at the turn of the nineteenth century. The Grand Junction stretched for over 90 miles, with its source at the Thames in Brentford. From here it forged a path mainly through Hertfordshire until it joined the Oxford Canal.

In 1929, it was decided to merge the Grand Junction with other canals to form one stretch of waterway. The result was a canal that linked the great rivers of England, including the Trent and the Thames, to many areas of Southern England and, most importantly, the more industrial centres in the Midlands. Today, these canals have ceased to be the important trade link with the cities that they once were, and concentrate mainly on providing pleasure trips through some of the most picturesque countryside in England.

River Dee
CHESTER CHESHIRE

The origins of many of England's large modern cities lie in their proximity to watercourses, which were essential in ancient times simply for survival and, in later centuries, for the success of trade, when travel by water was by far the quickest and simplest method of transporting goods. Attracted by its ideal situation on the River Dee, flowing from North Wales, the Romans formed a settlement here at Chester, from the small seeds of which a prosperous town has grown.

In medieval times, the port on the Dee proved to be a significant trade link with countries in Europe and with Ireland and Scotland. The success that this brought the town enhanced its status until it became one of the most important ports in the country. For over two hundred years, the Dee helped Chester thrive and expand, but in the fifteenth century the harbour started to silt up and the town's decline began. When it was eventually in a position to reassert its maritime control, it was too late. The opening of the Liverpool docks in 1715 meant that Chester could not compete with the young city, and it never regained its former status.

RIVER DERWENT
PEAK DISTRICT DERBYSHIRE

The River Derwent stretches over nearly 50 miles of the most beautiful and varied Derbyshire countryside, and is the longest river in the district. It begins its journey at Bleaklow and rushes southwards, through the three main reservoirs on the river – Howden, Derwent and Ladybower – a chain of water that is one of the central attractions along the river. Ultimately, the Derwent twists its way out of the Peak District and onwards towards Derby.

A variety of landscapes characterise the river's course. Some sections are calm and green, with hills gently rolling up on either side of the banks, but in other places the river takes in some of the most spectacular Tors and cliffs, including High Tor at Matlock. Along its length, patches of woodland stand with their glades lit by the sun, or containing dark shadows that cast ominous reflections in the water. Each area has its own character, and the river's own flow – smooth and slow or rough and wild – matches its surroundings. Along the banks of the Derwent, an abundance of mills stand, some of them still working, and other buildings revel in the additional beauty the river lends them. Most notably, the Derwent runs through the grounds of Chatsworth, the grandiose stately home of the Dukes of Devonshire.

Hambleden Mill on the Thames
HAMBLEDEN BUCKINGHAMSHIRE

The village of Hambleden is situated in the Chiltern Valley in Buckinghamshire near a stretch of the River Thames. From the village, an ancient road leads to Hambleden Mill. This beautiful timbered building has lorded over the banks of the Thames since the fourteenth century, when the river was an important resource for local people. Along the banks of the Thames in Buckinghamshire are many examples of old buildings and reminders of earlier English inhabitants. The Roman road that runs to the mill is just one of a number of ancient relics in this area, which include the fascinating remains of a settlement at Yewden.

Today, the mill is a picturesque addition to an already lovely area. Its white-painted exterior is reflected in the clear water of the river, and the roof is topped by a weathervane resting on a small turret. The stillness of the Thames in front of the mill belies the great power of the river elsewhere along its route, and this clear sheet of water suddenly drops in white foaming steps to the weir. This stretch of the Thames is also characterised by locks to control the water levels and aid the boats which frequent the river.

River Cam at the Backs
CAMBRIDGE CAMBRIDGESHIRE

Like many other large cities in England, Cambridge started its life as a small Roman settlement on the banks of a river that was then known as the Granta. Today the waters of this river still delight the inhabitants of the city, and the tourists that flock here, alike. Now rechristened the Cam, this enchanting river is a delightful addition to the charms of the city. Meandering along an unhurried path through the green lawns and hills that dominate the countryside, the banks of the Cam are a paradise for those who enjoy riverside walks, or who delight in sitting along its shady banks, taking in the scenery.

The Cam avoids the bustling city centre, and runs along one edge behind the stretch of colleges. The area pictured here is known as the Backs and lies behind King's College and Trinity Hall. Within this stretch are three bridges, and further upriver lies the elegant honey-coloured arch of the Cam's famous Bridge of Sighs. This part of the river is a particular attraction for those wishing to participate in the punting or rowing activities that are an essential part of Cambridge life. On the opposite side of the river lie the two beautiful Fellows Gardens associated with these two major colleges.

Rydal Water
THE LAKE DISTRICT CUMBRIA

Situated on the banks of the River Rothay, the village of Rydal is perhaps best known for its association with the poet William Wordsworth, who moved to Rydal Mount from his home in Grassmere in 1813. He lived here until his death in 1850. Rydal has other literary associations as well, most notably with the poet Matthew Arnold, whose memorial can be found in the small church in the village. Like many other lakeland areas, Rydal was a place of inspiration for poets, writers and painters, due to its unique beauty and air of solitude and peace.

Rydal Water lies just to the west of this charming village. It is a small lake, stretching one mile in length and only a quarter of a mile across, at the foot of the magnificent Rydal Fell. The River Rothay flows out from Rydal Water and on into the most famous of all the Cumbrian lakes, Windermere. Surrounded by a landscape of intense greenery and woodland, scattered with picturesque cottages, there is marvellous walking to be had around the Water. As one of the smallest lakes in the district, it is especially popular in winter, when it quickly freezes over, providing an outdoor skating rink amidst the spectacular scenery.

River Thames
CLIFTON HAMPDEN OXFORDSHIRE

The Thames is, by virtue of its length and situation running through the country's capital, the most important river in England. The source of this magnificent and changeable river lies in the Cotswold Hills in Gloucestershire, where four streams – the Isis, the Churn, the Leach and the Coln – meet and flow down to Oxford. From here, the river runs south-eastwards towards Reading, and on to London, where the wide expanse of water divides the city in two parts, south and north of the river. Out of London it flows between Essex and Kent into the North Sea.

The river flows through some of the most beautiful scenery in southern England, and scattered along its banks are numerous attractive villages and towns, all of which have relied on the water of the Thames for many centuries for energy and industry. Along these routes the river is extremely diverse, at times forming only a narrow, meandering path that is calm and beautiful, while in other places it is a fast-flowing rush of foaming waters. It is in London, however, that it is at its most impressive, where over 30 miles of the river are taken up by the famous docks, and dominated by sea craft of all shapes and types.

River Dove
DOVEDALE DERBYSHIRE

This breathtaking area of the country forms part of the Peak District National Park, an area of incredible beauty and diverse scenery. The harsh limestone rocks are tempered by areas of lush rolling hills and rich farmland, amongst which rivers meander and lakes shimmer. Dovedale marks the boundary between Staffordshire and Derbyshire, and its striking splendour has long made it one of the most popular parts of the Peak District.

Izaak Walton, the renowned author of *The Compleat Angler* thought the Dove one of the most lovely rivers in England. The abundance of trout that inhabit the waters attract fishermen from all over the country, but this is only a small part of its appeal. Forging its way through a dramatic landscape of limestone walls, its path runs for approximately three miles. The ravines that lie on either side are made up of a series of rock formations, weathered by the elements into curious shapes and patterns. Christened with romantic names such as the Twelve Apostles and Lover's Leap, these add to the mysterious beauty of Dovedale. By the side of the gorges many impressive caves and gullies can be found, carved into the rock by the relentless flow of the river.

Linton Falls
GRASSINGTON NORTH YORKSHIRE

Linton is one of the most beautiful and traditional villages that the Yorkshire Dales has to offer. Situated a short walk across fields from the larger village of Grassington, the Falls lie on the outskirts of the village. As one crosses the bridge, the river crashes down a series of steps, creating small waterfalls. The musical sound of the water rushing along its course harmonises with the cries of the lapwings that inhabit this area. This perfect scene is complemented by the small church that lies on the opposite bank at the bend of the river.

Linton is a typical Dales village: a group of houses clustered around a picturesque village pond, cobbled streets and marvellous surrounding countryside. It is unusual, however, in that it is home to a number of almshouses. These were funded from a bequest left by Richard Fountaine, a seventeenth-century entrepreneur, who made his fortune as a timber merchant during the Plague and in the aftermath of the Great Fire of London in 1666. These houses still stand largely in their original state, forming an unusual and curious part of the village.

River Windrush

LOWER SLAUGHTER GLOUCESTERSHIRE

The River Windrush winds its way through the two small villages of Upper and Lower Slaughter – whose unappealing names actually derive from the Anglo Saxon for 'marshy place'. The river is the most attractive feature of these two beautifully undisturbed Gloucestershire villages. Along its route, typical village houses, made from golden limestone stand quietly, a charming addition to the scene. The villages grew up in the sixteenth century, when the stone building industry was prospering, and as such, many of these houses have stone roofs, gables and window surrounds. This is characteristic of Cotswold houses, where the local stone was freely available. It has come to be one of the most familiar features of this part of the country.

As the Windrush meanders under small stone bridges, many other beautiful buildings can be seen along its banks, particularly the old corn mill at Lower Slaughter, which dates from the nineteenth century, and which once made use of the river for power. Its waterwheel is still completely intact. Together, these unprepossessing but enchanting features make up a landscape that has attracted many artists to record and preserve their typical English beauty.

Oxford Canal
NAPTON WARWICKSHIRE

England's earliest inhabitants, built towns along the banks of the country's plentiful rivers, to provide access for building materials and to provide links with other trading centres inland. The rivers were exploited in this way for many centuries, but the same problems endured throughout. River courses were erratic, often taking laborious winding routes, and there was no way to control the water levels; floods and droughts often made transportation difficult.

A plan was devised to create a network of man-made rivers that took direct routes between the important trading centres, and water levels could be controlled by the use of locks and weirs. These would connect with the rivers where suitable and run their own man-made paths wherever the natural watercourses became problematic. The implementation of this idea sowed the seeds that would eventually fertilise the Industrial Revolution.

The Oxford Canal was just one of these artificial waterways. Connecting with the old Grand Junction Canal, the Oxford forged a path southwards towards the city that bears its name. Sadly, these ingeniously designed and beautifully constructed canals were not to enjoy a long period of commercial use. The introduction of the steam railways in the later eighteenth century rendered them virtually obsolete, but they remain a scenic and enjoyable reminder of the country's past.

River Wye
MONSAL DALE DERBYSHIRE

The most significant feature of Monsal Dale is its famous viaduct, which is an unexpected sign of human encroachment upon the impressive landscape. Almost completely hidden by the trees and hills that stretch up on either side of it, the viaduct across the River Wye was built in 1863 when steam railways were at the height of their prosperity. Although some people resented the destruction of the area's natural beauty, disused lines like this are now a haunting testimony to the great age of steam, and fragments of the line can be seen all over the landscape.

Monsal Dale remains one of the most bewitching parts of the Peak District, a picturesque hamlet nestling at the foot of great limestone hills scattered with small areas of woodland. The Wye is its most beautiful natural feature, though. It is a pleasant, unhurried river, flowing calmly through the villages, like Monsal Dale, that have grown up along its banks. The walks along the valley by the riverside afford some of the best views of the countryside between the larger commercial towns of Bakewell and Buxton.

River Thurne
THURNE DYKE NORFOLK

The Thurne is one of the three main rivers that run through the heart of the beautiful Norfolk Broads. At Breydon Water, the Thurne joins the Yare and the Bure in a marvellous amalgamation, which then flows down to Great Yarmouth and into the sea. Along its route, many small streams meander alongside the river, cutting shimmering paths through the marshy lands. In places where the rivers widen, large lakes are formed, and it is these that are known as the 'broads'. Their size once led people to believe that they were natural lakes, but they are in fact just a continuation of the rivers flowing uninterrupted to their destination.

In all, the three rivers make up 125 miles of graceful waterway, making this an extremely popular area for boating. Almost the whole stretch is navigable by boats and is unhindered by any locks, making for a pleasant and smooth ride through some of the area's loveliest countryside. Its pleasant situation and peaceful atmosphere also attracts many anglers who come to reap the harvest of fish that inhabit the still waters of the river.

RIVER STOUR
CHRISTCHURCH DORSET

This picture, taken at Tuckton Bridge in Christchurch depicts the small mooring area of the River Stour. The fishing boats illustrate the important commercial aspect of this and many other rivers like it throughout the country, although the economies of many coastal counties like Dorset are being supported increasingly by the growing tourist trade as well as by fishing. Waterways like the Stour play their part in this essential business.

The river provides an attractive spectacle, meandering through this beautiful Dorset town and into Christchurch Bay. The buildings of the town provide a fascinating complement to the River Stour. The most illustrious of these is the parish church – a title that belies its massive proportions and great history. The church is the only remaining part of an old Norman structure that has stood on this spot for many centuries. In 1539, however, the priory of which it formed a part, was torn down as a result of the large scale Dissolution. The priory church was left standing only because of its use as the parish church.

River Severn
TEWKESBURY GLOUCESTERSHIRE

The River Severn dominates the landscape of south-western England. From its source in the Plynlimon Mountains in Wales, it travels in an easterly direction into England, where it turns southwards towards Bristol. It is here that the river is at its most spectacular, a broad stretch of water dividing England and Wales, which eventually widens out into the Bristol Channel. This stretch is approximately 200 miles in length, and it is possible to travel along most of this without difficulty.

The tributaries of the Severn include the Avon and the Wye, and all year round in the Severn regions, fishermen can be seen fishing for the trout that abound in its waters. The Severn itself is noted for its salmon. Other waterways also run into this long river at various points along its course. The revolution in canal building meant that the Severn, along with the other major rivers in the South, was connected to a network of artificial waterways which in turn linked it with the Thames, the Trent and the Mersey rivers.

Lake Windermere
AMBLESIDE CUMBRIA

Windermere is the most famous and arguably the most beautiful of all the Cumbrian lakes. At ten and a half miles long, it is the longest lake in England, and although its width for the most part matches its length, in places it is extremely narrow. Because of its size and its popularity with tourists, it can be difficult to appreciate the full splendour of this magnificent body of water with the plethora of boats of all shapes and sizes that dominate the surface, particularly throughout the summer months. Its setting, however, is undeniably enchanting. Unlike the heavy purple and grey crags that tower above the landscape in other parts of the Lake District, the area around Windermere – and particularly here at Ambleside – is softer and more green, with lovely areas of woodland and wild flowers.

All around the lake, birds make their nests along the banks of the water. In the grasses and fields not far away wild animals make their homes, and varied plantlife can be found. It is a paradise for walkers, and for those who simply want to soak up the scenery and the tranquil atmosphere.

HISTORIC ENGLAND

All over the country, in towns and villages, on hillsides and in coastal regions, lie remnants of England's ancient history. All serve as a reminder of some of its greatest events and as a testimony to its heroes.

Glastonbury Abbey
GLASTONBURY SOMERSET

The ruins of the Abbey at Glastonbury, and its famous nearby Tor, are steeped in myths and legends. The area's association with King Arthur has long been discussed and debated. It is believed to be the legendary Isle of Avalon, where Arthur went after receiving his fatal wound in his last great battle. It is also reputed to have been the burial place of the Holy Grail: the cup containing the blood of Christ that the Knights of the Round Table went in quest of in the most famous of the Arthurian legends.

Glastonbury is the oldest Christian site in England, with origins dating back to the Celts in the fourth century. Various monastic communities have made their bases here, including one founded by the West Saxon king, Ine. The Normans erected a church here in the early part of the twelfth century, but this was gutted by fire in 1184. In succeeding centuries, Glastonbury was periodically restored and expanded until the sixteenth century, when even its long and illustrious past could not save it from the undiscriminating Dissolution. Henry VIII had the monastery destroyed and the abbot executed on Glastonbury Tor. Since then, the Abbey has fallen into the mysterious but attractive ruin it is today, an evocative testimony to England's history.

Shakespeare's Birthplace
STRATFORD-UPON-AVON WARWICKSHIRE

The town of Stratford-upon-Avon owes its prosperity mainly to the fact that William Shakespeare was born here. His house is now open to the public, and the town itself abounds with monuments, theatres housing his plays, and numerous other testimonies to England's greatest literary figure.

The house was built in the late 1400s, and was originally two adjoining buildings. Shakespeare's father John bought the second house in 1556, and eventually connected the two and extended them to include a new section at the back. They are typical Tudor houses with timber frames, and as such they are susceptible to fire. For this reason the other houses in Henley Street that would have been part of the row in Shakespeare's time have since been demolished to preserve these two.

The house remained undisturbed until 1769, when the bedroom on the first floor was identified as the actual room in which Shakespeare was born, prompting a revival of interest in the building. The interior still reflects the way it would have looked during Shakespeare's lifetime, and the garden at the back has now been planted up with many of the trees and shrubs that are mentioned in his plays.

Stonehenge
SALISBURY WILTSHIRE

For centuries, Stonehenge has presented archaeologists with a number of mysterious paradoxes. It is known that the first stage of construction took place around 3000 BC, when the massive bank and ditch were created, and the first stone placed at the entrance. Later additions were made in 2100 BC, with the first circle of approximately eighty stones, and in 1500 BC when the impressive trilithons – two upright blocks with a lintel stone – were laid to complete the circle, as well as the half circle of stones which stands inside.

The trilithons and horseshoe stones were made from sandstone which came from the Marlborough Downs, but the earlier blocks were hewn from dolerite, or bluestone, which was sourced in the Welsh mountains. Some theories suggest that they were carried here to the Salisbury Plains by a glacier, but there is no evidence to support this idea. It is possible that they were actually quarried in the mountains and carried here by rafts, but this would have been an immense task. The other great mystery that shrouds Stonehenge is its purpose. It has been considered variously as a site of pagan ritual and worship, a palace, and some form of primitive calendar. These unanswered questions lend an air of intrigue to the most marvellous of all the prehistoric relics that lie scattered throughout the British Isles.

Tower of London
THE CITY LONDON

The Tower of London is probably the best-known historical monument in England, its long and bloody past lending it an air of mystery and fascination. The oldest part of the building is the White Tower which dates from 1078, the time of William the Conqueror. Today this tower is home to the Armoury and St John's Chapel, the oldest Norman church in London, as many of its contemporaries were destroyed in the Great Fire of 1666.

The role of the Tower has involved use as a stronghold, a royal palace and, most notoriously, a prison. Some of the most famous names in English history have been incarcerated here. Many never came out alive, including Guy Fawkes, Sir Thomas More and the Princes in the Tower. Among the luckier people to have spent time here is Sir Walter Raleigh, who, during his thirteen-year imprisonment wrote his *History of the World*. The White Tower stands on Tower Green, the infamous site of many executions, including those of two of Henry VIII's wives and Lady Jane Grey. Today two of the most popular attractions are the Crown Jewels which are housed here, and the Beefeaters who parade the Tower in their traditional costumes.

Statue of St Aidan
HOLY ISLAND NORTHUMBERLAND

In AD 635 Oswald, the king of Northumbria, decided to establish a priory on the island of Lindisfarne, now known as Holy Island, to spread the word of Christianity to his subjects who continued to worship according to the ancient pagan customs. He chose Aidan, a monk from the Scottish island of Iona, to lead this mission.

Aidan became the first Bishop of Lindisfarne, teaching by his own example of physical and spiritual purity, and under his guidance the priory became a prominent centre of Christianity, spreading the Word across northern England. It is said that on the night Aidan died, a shepherd boy tending his sheep in

the Scottish hills saw a host of angels in the sky surrounded by a blinding light, carrying the saint's soul towards heaven. This shepherd boy was later to become St Aidan's most influential successor, St Cuthbert.

Nothing remains of the original priory, but a marvellous sandstone church built in Norman times stands on the island, and it remains a place of pilgrimage. Holy Island is only accessible from the mainland when the tides are favourable, but this remoteness enhances the atmosphere of sanctity and peacefulness that still surrounds the island.

HMS Victory

PORTSMOUTH HAMPSHIRE

'England expects that every man this day will do his duty'. These inspirational words spoken by Lord Nelson as he set off on his flagship *HMS Victory* for the Battle of Trafalgar are now legendary. This was to become one of the most famous battles in English history, making a hero of Lord Nelson.

HMS Victory had already enjoyed forty years of active service by the time she set sail on 14 September 1805 and, despite the damage this battle inflicted, she continued for a further twenty years. Built in 1765, the *Victory* was 60 metres from bow to stern, and was loaded up with more than 100 canons. During the battle, these were to ensure the success of the English, but they could not save the Admiral's life. In the confusion of the battle, Nelson was shot by a French sniper, and a few hours later he died in the arms of his officer Hardy, in a scene that was to become the imaginative subject of art and literature for many years. Unusually, Nelson had not wanted to be buried at sea, so his body was preserved in a barrel of brandy, until he eventually received a state funeral at St Paul's Cathedral, where a memorial to this great man can still be seen.

Roman Baths
BATH AVON

The healing properties of these springs are reputed to have been discovered around 500 BC by the father of the infamous King Lear, Prince Bladud. Suffering from leprosy, he was banished from his own court, and became a swineherd. One day he noticed that certain of his pigs' skin diseases appeared to be improved and even cured by rolling in the mud and puddles created by the springs, so he decided to try it for himself. He was cured of his leprosy, and returned to court, where he eventually became king.

It was the Romans, however, who first turned Bath into a famous spa town, constructing a number of grand buildings to house the baths. After the Romans left Britain, these magnificent structures were left to decay, and only saw a revival in fortunes at the turn of the eighteenth century, when they were visited by Queen Anne. They instantly became a fashionable attraction once more, drawing the rich and famous to take the waters. The ancient springs contain over forty minerals and still maintain a constant temperature of 46.5°C. The buildings themselves remain an awe-inspiring sight, a complex design of pillars and walkways, with rooms for bathing and cooling off, and many other wonderful relics of the Roman era.

Hadrian's Wall
HOUSESTEADS NORTHUMBERLAND

Hadrian's Wall is the most impressive of all the legacies left by the Romans in England. Begun in AD 122, the seventy-five mile stretch of the wall runs from Carlisle to Newcastle, and was designed as a fortification against attack. It was also a means of controlling passage in and out of the province and in its time it was extended and changed on a number of occasions. At one point it was abandoned altogether and a new wall begun that was to run between the Firths of Forth and Clyde, but Hadrian's Wall was later recommissioned and remained the boundary of the Roman Empire until the fifth century.

Constructed of local stone, the wall is characterised by a series of forts and towers at carefully measured intervals along its length, and it was reinforced by a massive ditch – the Vallum – on its north side, traces of which still remain. It is estimated that the wall once stood at approximately six metres high and at its widest it would have been about three metres thick. In later times, parts of the wall were removed and used for building blocks, but although parts of it are now missing and its original immense proportions are lost forever, it remains an incredible testimony to the ingenuity and strength of the Roman people.

Roman Fort on Hadrian's Wall
HOUSESTEADS NORTHUMBERLAND

There were originally between seventeen and nineteen forts situated at intervals along the stretch of Hadrian's Wall, and between each one are milecastles and towers which were used as lookout points. Each of these forts could hold between 500 and 1000 men, both infantry and cavalry, and their strategic locations meant that trouble could be observed from a great distance and defences prepared for any attack. Within the forts, buildings were constructed to serve as barracks for the soldiers, administrative centres and storerooms, making them fairly self-contained.

When the wall was first constructed, a number of forts which lay to the south were built, but during construction, plans were changed and it was decided to incorporate these fortifications into the wall itself. The Vallum – the great ditch around the outside of the wall to serve as an extra defence measure – was accessed from the forts by walkways. Later on, around the second century AD, a military road was built to provide easy access for the soldiers from one site to another along the wall. Today, little remains of these great strongholds, although in one or two areas, most notably at Housesteads, the foundation stones lying undisturbed explain the ancient structures and tactics the Romans used.

Statue of King Alfred
WANTAGE OXFORDSHIRE

The lovely village of Wantage lays claim to being the birthplace of Alfred the Great, one of the most significant of England's early monarchs, who ruled from AD 871–899. Constantly under threat of dominance by Danish invaders, Alfred realised the importance of co-habiting with them rather than fighting to the death. He therefore established a border marking his own territories, separate from the northern Danish domains. He instigated many reforms within the country, and had a great influence on the revival of learning and scholarship that occurred at this time, writing many works of his own. It is also possible that he had a hand in planning the well-known *Anglo-Saxon Chronicle*, which dates from his reign. When Alfred died he left the country in a much stronger position than when he had first ascended.

Wantage saw the birth of the king in AD 849, and this statue stands in the centre of the village market place, a testimony to the area's most important figure. Statues and memorials pay tribute to King Alfred all over England, particularly marking the sites of some of his great battles with the Danes.

Churchill's Grave
BLADON OXFORDSHIRE

The grave of Sir Winston Churchill lies in Bladon, near Blenheim Palace. This great man was undeniably the most prominent politician in England in the twentieth century. Born in 1874, he was only twenty-six when he gained his first seat in Parliament, and this was to be the start of a long and illustrious career.

His position as First Lord of the Admiralty from 1911, meant that he was responsible for preparing the British fleet against the Germans on the eve of the First World War. Later, in the shocked aftermath of 1918, he was made Minister of War. Between the Wars, Churchill held a number of positions in the government, but at the outbreak of the Second World War, he was reinstated as First Lord of the Admiralty. A year later, he became Prime Minister of Great Britain. Many people have attributed Britain's success in the War to Churchill's determination and leadership abilities, and there can be no doubt that he certainly played a significant role in the victory. Churchill will always be closely associated with modern English history, his face and his voice – in the days before television – have become inextricably linked with England's darkest hours and its greatest achievements.

Village Stocks
ALDBURY HERTFORDSHIRE

These stocks which stand by the village pond at Aldbury are a fascinating and picturesque reminder of the old practices that were upheld as part of traditional village life. If local people committed crimes that affected the village, they were often sentenced by the local authorities to a term in the stocks. This normally ranged from a few hours, sometimes stretching to days. Their legs were locked into the wooden contraption so they could not move. Not only was this considered appropriate as a means of publicly humiliating the offender, but fellow villagers could also punish them by throwing things at them, or spitting on them. Few examples of this form of punishment are found in their original setting, because being made of wood, many have decayed over time.

Aldbury, where these stocks have been carefully preserved as a great local attraction, is a typical English village, with groups of houses clustered around the village pond. Its great beauty has made it popular with film and television crews who often use it as the quintessential English village.

Statue of Lady Godiva
COVENTRY WEST MIDLANDS

Lady Godiva has become the city of Coventry's most famous citizen, and this amusing local tale, which has become known throughout the country, is commemorated all over the city. Originating in the eleventh century, the story tells how the Earl of Mercia Leofric introduced a new policy of taxation to his subjects in the city. His wife, Lady Godiva, was so shocked by them she decided to protest. To ensure her husband noticed, however, and to demonstrate her support for them to the citizens, she decided to ride through the streets of Coventry naked. In deference to her position, and in fear of Leofric, all the people turned away as she passed – except one: Peeping Tom.

This statue, created by Reid Dick, was unveiled in 1949. It stands in the middle of Coventry's Broadgate, a large, open square in the heart of the city, and is one of the most notable monuments to the local legend. At the south end of the square is a clock upon which the story can be watched on the stroke of every hour, as Lady Godiva appears on horseback, with Peeping Tom peering through his window above.

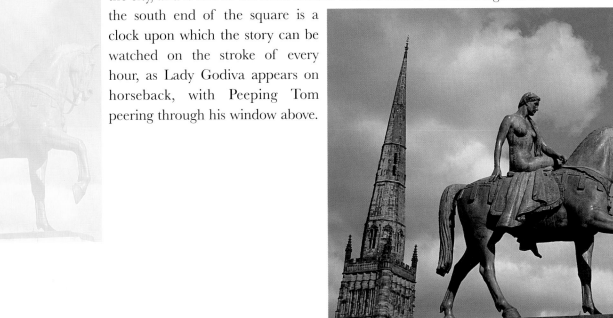

Donnington Castle
NEWBURY BERKSHIRE

Donnington castle is a romantic ruin situated in Newbury, dating from the fourteenth century. It is now most famous for the two significant battles that took place nearby during the English Civil War. The first occurred in 1643 and the second the following year. Neither of the battles proved decisive in the final outcome of the War, but these events, together with the haunting remains of the old gatehouse, have provided Newbury with a sense of history that is reflected in the town's museum, where relics from the era can be found.

Newbury was once a major cloth-manufacturing area as far back as the fifteenth century. John Smallwood, one of the leaders of the trade at that time, played an important role in the famous Battle of Flodden in 1513, where the armies of Henry VIII and James IV fought for supremacy over Scotland. Smallwood led a company of 150 men into the battle, and he too is commemorated around the town. Today, Newbury is best-known for its racecourse, which draws hundreds of enthusiasts every week to indulge the English love of all equestrian events.

Horse Guards
WHITEHALL LONDON

For over 200 years Whitehall has been home to all the main government buildings in London. This wide and majestic street runs between Trafalgar Square and Parliament Square in the centre of the city, and is dotted with statues and monuments. It also housed London's main royal home, Whitehall Palace, but a fire in 1698 destroyed most of this and many of the other fine buildings that once stood here. All that remains of the palace today is the Banqueting House, designed by Inigo Jones.

Horse Guards is situated on the old tournament ground used by Henry VIII, and the building with its uniformed guards is a favourite attraction in London. The officers are chosen from the Queen's Life Guard and consist of two cavalrymen on their mounts and one infantry soldier. All three are dressed in their ceremonial uniforms, and must stand to attention for up to two hours at a time. The Changing of the Guard takes place every morning at 11.00 am, when twelve mounted guards ride from their barracks in Hyde Park to Whitehall for the official ceremony.

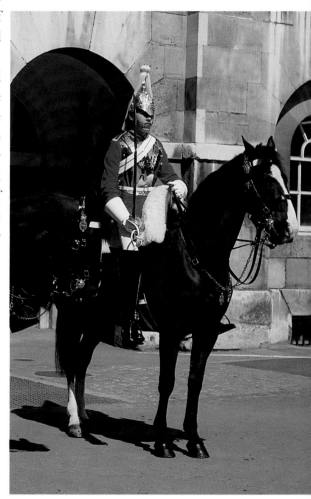

TRADITION & CULTURE

Through the ages, the customs and traditions of the English have endured, to reveal a proud sense of the country's past and to give the land an amazingly rich cultural inheritance.

Morris Dancing
BAMPTON OXFORDSHIRE

It is believed that the tradition of morris dancing has its roots in Elizabethan times, when colourful entertainments such as this were extremely popular in the courts of the wealthy. Exactly where the idea came from is unknown, but it is possible that the English adapted the customary dances of the Moors in the east into their own form of amusement. In these times, the dancing took a different form to the kind we are familiar with today, and was generally part of a pageant or play. Eventually morris dancing evolved into an integral part of the traditional Mayday celebrations that were popular throughout the seventeenth and eighteenth centuries.

Today morris dancing still holds a great appeal. The lively and colourful dances, characterised by bells attached to the legs, coloured ribbons and laces, and the waving of white handkerchiefs, are performed on public holidays in villages throughout England, and many places have their own morris dancing societies. Such scenes reflect the love the English have of celebration, and their determination to honour their history and customs.

Royal Shakespeare Theatre
STRATFORD-UPON-AVON WARWICKSHIRE

The original Shakespeare Memorial Theatre was built in 1879, and housed all the bard's plays for nearly 50 years until a fire reduced it to ruins in the 1920s. The new Memorial Theatre was created by Elizabeth Scott, after a competition was held to find the right designer for this prestigious venue. The building was completed in 1932, and has become the permanent home of the Royal Shakespeare Company in Stratford. The exterior of the building is notably decorated with six carved figures representing Love, Life, Death, War, Faithlessness and Mirth – appropriate symbols for the themes that run through the plays of Shakespeare.

The Memorial Theatre was closely followed by another, The Swan, which stands close by on the banks of the river. Between them, these two theatres draw crowds of thousands every month to Stratford. Surprisingly, little attention was paid to the town for over a century after Shakespeare's death. It was only when an actor and theatre manager from London came to Stratford and showed an interest in Shakespeare's house, identifying one of the bedrooms as the room in which he had been born, that interest was aroused in the town. It has since expanded and prospered, revelling in the glory of being the home of England's greatest literary son.

Student Bicycles
OXFORD OXFORDSHIRE

Oxford is one of the longest serving and most renowned university cities in the world. This ancient seat of learning still maintains many traditions and customs that have long since been abandoned elsewhere, and its highly selective process of admission has made it one of the two most exclusive and sought after universities in England. The rivalry – particularly in sporting matters – between Oxford and its counterpart Cambridge is well known, and the pinnacle of this competition comes every year with the Varsity boat race along the Thames.

This magnificent city is a maze of outstanding buildings and impressive architecture, most of which are part of the university administration units and the world-famous colleges which lie scattered around Oxford. There can be no doubt that this is a student city: the ancient feel of intense scholarship combines with all the attributes of young modern life to create a warm, studious, but fun-loving atmosphere, one that complements a visitor's sense of awe at the history that exudes from every building. One of the most enduring images of Oxford is that of a multitude of bicycles such as these, which are used by the students and the locals as an effective and environmentally-friendly way of getting around the city.

Village Cricket
WEST ILSLEY BERKSHIRE

Many English villages have managed to resist the advances of urban development enough to retain their own unique atmosphere. Most of the smaller villages have an air of warmth and hospitality, welcoming to strangers and on friendly terms with their neighbours. These places are often characterised by a few small cottages huddled cosily around a green or a pond, with populations numbering only a few inhabitants. It is mainly in the villages that the old traditions and customs are perpetuated, where a strong sense of community is an important part of everyday life.

The traditional village cricket match like the one pictured here has become an English institution. In the summer months, the men from the villages and the surrounding area gather on the green or in a nearby field to play this very English game. It is one of the few times that a friendly rivalry supersedes the usual pleasantries. The cricket matches are a community affair, and most residents will gather to watch, while the women prepare the customary Cricket Tea.

Eights Week on the Isis
OXFORD OXFORDSHIRE

The Isis is not, as one might believe, a river in its own right, but is actually the name given to the section of the Thames that runs through the city of Oxford. The river is the city's central attraction and an important part of Oxford life. Boat trips on the river remain popular with tourists and locals, punting being a favourite pastime. These small narrow boats echo the romanticism of the Venetian gondolas, as they are propelled with the use of a long pole. The waters of the Isis, and its neighbouring river here in Oxford, the Cherwell, are very shallow, and therefore ideal for this leisurely method of transportation.

It was this stretch of water that played host to the very first Oxford and Cambridge Boat Race in 1829. Although the Varsity race now takes place in London, the Oxford team – along with other members of the University rowing fraternity – can often be seen practising along the Isis. Other races are still held here, the most famous of which is the Eights. Held annually at the end of May, this draws crowds of people from Oxford and further afield to watch the rowing tournament from the banks of the river.

Cowes Week
COWES ISLE OF WIGHT

Cowes is the centre of yachting activity on the Isle of Wight. All year round sailing fanatics flock to the town to participate in the weekend regattas or to enjoy themselves at the yacht club functions.

The success of Cowes as a yachting paradise began in 1820, when the Prince Regent offered his patronage to the Royal Yacht Squadron here. Today, this exclusive society has its headquarters in the magnificent castle that was built by Henry VIII as a fortification against invasion from the Spanish and the French. The area's historical importance was enhanced in the 1950s when the first trial runs of the newly-invented hovercraft were made at Cowes.

The highlight of the year, however, is Cowes Week, which begins on the first weekend in August. This world-famous festival attracts people not only from the island and mainland Britain, but from all over the world, who come to watch the colourful sailing regatta, drawn by the prestige of the event and the high-society atmosphere. Many other important races and events are held at other times, though, including the Round the Island race in June, and the Admiral's Cup, which only takes place every two years.

Maypole Dancing
KINTBURY BERKSHIRE

The origins of this ancient custom go back many centuries, when most villages would have had a maypole. On the first day of May, the villagers would gather on the green and celebrate the arrival of Spring by performing dances around the pole, in the manner of ancient ritual. The addition of the coloured ribbons occurred much later, probably in the nineteenth century, when the idea was inspired by ballet performances where ribbons were used to graceful and colourful effect.

The poles can stand up to three metres high, and ribbons are attached to the top in groups of four. The dancers form two circles, one inside the other, around the maypole, holding on to the end of the ribbons, and dance around it, weaving in and out of each other, creating patterns to traditional folk music. Some of the dances are quite simple and elegant, forming criss-cross patterns, others are more complicated and create intricate twists and plaits around the pole. Although this custom has experienced a decline in recent years, some villages still uphold these mayday customs, and maypole dancing is popular in schools.

Heavy Horse Ploughing Contest
FINSTOCK OXFORDSHIRE

This photograph shows contestants participating in the annual West of England Heavy Horse Ploughing Contest at Finstock. This marvellous tradition encourages one to reflect on the days before mechanisation, and involves a series of contests using these beautifully dressed heavy horses and small iron ploughs.

Agriculture remains an important industry in England, particularly in the west, where the landscape is composed of crop fields and fallow pastures dotted with farmhouses and livestock. The introduction of farm machinery such as ploughs was swept in with the tidal wave of the Industrial Revolution. The first ploughs were small wooden devices, which gradually had their wooden spikes replaced with ones made of iron. Iron spikes were more durable and certainly more effective in tilling the soil. In the early nineteenth century, the first plough made completely of iron was invented in the United States, and since this time, farming has moved on in leaps and bounds. Mechanical farm machinery has made earning a living from the land a great deal easier than in the days when these horses and ploughs were commonly used.

Punch and Judy
WEYMOUTH DORSET

The traditional Punch and Judy show is the oldest form of English seaside entertainment. For over four hundred years the familiar figures of Mr Punch, his wife Judy and the policeman have played their parts in their striped-tent theatres in resorts all over the country. The traditional story runs that Judy leaves Punch at home with the baby, which cries so he throws it down the stairs. When the long-suffering Judy comes home and finds the baby, she attacks Punch with a stick, but he beats her, and throws her down the stairs too. The policeman who comes to investigate gets the same treatment. Although, the horror of the story and the violence of Mr Punch have been brought into question in recent years, they still remain popular attractions.

Weymouth beach, where this Punch and Judy show takes place, was brought to prominence by George III, who began the craze of sea-bathing in this area. It was a fashion that was adopted by most members of the upper classes. Today, the buildings along the sea front reflect the town's Georgian affluence, and Weymouth retains its popularity as one of Dorset's favourite resorts.

Skidby Mill
BEVERLEY HUMBERSIDE

The old market town of Beverley is characterised by its plethora of listed buildings. The maze of small cobbled streets and alleyways contain hundreds of marvellous examples of Georgian and Victorian architecture. Its two main attractions, however, are the churches that stand there: the Minster and St Mary's Church. All Beverley's buildings reflect a time when the town was at the height of its prosperity as a successful wool-trading centre.

Not far from Beverley lies the little village of Skidby, nestling in the protection of the East Yorkshire Wolds, on the banks of the Humber River. It is here that the area's chief attraction lies, near the Humber Bridge. Skidby Mill is the last intact mill in this part of the country. Constructed in 1821, Skidby Mill still produces flour in the same way it did a century ago. It dominates the horizon as a striking landmark, with its white sails and domed crown a neat contrast to the black tower. Today the mill is the property of the Beverley Borough Council, and visitors can take a step back in time by visiting it to see how flour used to be produced, when mills such as this were common sights over the countryside.

Regent Street
WEST END LONDON

Regent Street was designed as part of John Nash's master plan for this area of London. It was a plan which included the magnificent Regent's Park, and many other of London's most popular features today. Regent Street was intended to be the first of a series of avenues that would lead to the park, characterised by shops and desirable residences for the well to-do of the city.

Today, with Oxford Street which lies to its north, Regent Street forms part of the busiest shopping area in London. Crowded with chain stores and more exclusive shops, Regent Street is always bustling. Its most famous store is Hamley's, the world's largest toy shop, which boasts floor after floor of every conceivable toy and game. The shop is especially impressive at Christmas, when the larger Regent Street stores vie with each other to produce the most innovative window displays. These works of modern art are enhanced by the famous Regent Street Illuminations. The miles of fairy lights are now a familiar feature in the winter months in central London, adding an air of festivity and brilliance to the grey of the city.

The Waverley Paddle Steamer
BOURNEMOUTH DORSET

The *Waverley* is the last sea-going paddle steamer in the world. This picture was taken when the boat left her home in the north to travel to Bournemouth. She docked at Bournemouth Pier, one of two piers along this stretch of beach in Dorset, and one that has facilities for launching cruises and for fishing in the waters that swirl around it.

Paddle steam ships like the *Waverley* began to thrive at the beginning of the nineteenth century, after a method of creating steam power by use of a wheel was discovered. For many years, paddle steamers were used on the canals and rivers of inland England. The first ever transatlantic crossing by one of these boats occurred in 1819, when the *Savannah* embarked from Georgia and finally docked at Liverpool. It was not until 1840, however, that a permanent shuttle across the Atlantic between the two countries was established. These crossings were made by large wooden vessels with paddle wheels like the *Waverley*, and many also used sails for propulsion when the winds were favourable. Eventually, of course, developments rendered the magnificent steamers obsolete and they were replaced by faster, more efficient fuel-powered crafts.

Severn Valley Railway
ARLEY HEREFORD & WORCESTER

Running 16 miles from Kidderminster to Bridgnorth, the Severn Valley Railway is a little piece of history that has been lovingly maintained. The steam engines wind their way through the small stations that have been preserved in the splendour of their hey-day.

The first steam train was built in 1804, but its was not until the famous Rocket was designed by George Stephenson that a blueprint for the future of steam locomotion was created. This made its first trip between Manchester and Liverpool in 1829. The impact this invention had on commercial activity in Britain was incredible – the most important event in an age that saw the culmination of the Industrial Revolution at the end of the nineteenth century.

The significance the introduction of the steam engine had on English history is reflected in the number of small railways scattered all over the country that still employ these trains. Now mainly tourist attractions, railways like the Severn Valley can take one on a journey to the past. The luxurious nature of the trains – particularly in these days of crowded, uncomfortable carriages in fast but arguably ugly machines – is a delight to experience, and the lovely countryside that can be enjoyed along the way is an added bonus.

Traditional Teashop
GODSHILL ISLE OF WIGHT

The pride of Godshill village is its small Church of the Lily Cross. It takes its name from a painting that hangs inside depicting the crucified Christ on a three-branched lily. The painting dates from the fifteenth century, and is a beautiful and thought-provoking feature of this fine church.

In keeping with its attraction to visitors, the village streets are lined with teashops like this one: a traditional part of village trade. Small, 'olde-worlde' shops selling refreshments such as cream teas are a familiar

sight in villages and small towns all over England, particularly in the rural parts of Yorkshire and the West Country. Although Godshill now offers many other attractions – including a model village – designed to tempt the tourist away from the beaches and large towns on the island, the village's real fascination is less contrived. This is rooted in its simple beauty. The streets are lined with high walls, and scattered around, typical English cottages built of thatch and stone, with climbing roses and other plants and flowers, provide a beauty and charm that is purely English.

Fishing Boats
HASTINGS EAST SUSSEX

The town of Hastings is situated on the coast of the English Channel, and it was a flourishing port in ancient times. The name of Hastings is now known all over the world in connection with English history, as it was here that perhaps the most important battle ever fought on English soil took place – the Battle of Hastings.

William, the Duke of Normandy, asserted his claim to the English throne in 1066, when he landed at Hastings with his army on 28 September. A bitter battle ensued between the Duke and the English king Harold II, in which the king was defeated. From this time, William was nicknamed 'the Conqueror' and assumed the English crown as William I.

Hastings flourished as a thriving port for over 300 years, until the French raids left it in ruins. The town never recovered its previous status as a seafaring region. In the eighteenth century, its revival began, as it became a popular seaside resort. Today, it still maintains this attraction, and the great historical significance of the area draws crowds of people to visit the field where the great Battle of Hastings took place. The boats lying here on the beach are an apt reflection of the town's former affluence.

Harrods
KNIGHTSBRIDGE LONDON

Undoubtedly the most famous department store in England – perhaps in the world – the origins of Harrods are humble. In 1849 Henry Charles Harrod opened a small store selling groceries on the Brompton Road. This little shop prospered, and eventually expanded beyond its proprietor's wildest dreams.

Today, the Harrods empire is contained within the world-famous seven-storey building in Knightsbridge. Erected in 1905, this impressive red-brick construction is now owned by the Al Fayed family, and the

literally hundreds of departments, bars and restaurants that make up the shop are manned by an army of staff numbering thousands. In keeping with its upper-class image, there is a dress-code for shoppers wishing to enter the building and, once inside, the overwhelming maze of magnificently decorated halls sell just about anything one could wish for. At night, thousands of lights on the store's façade outline its vast proportions, converting it into an illuminated fairy-tale castle.

The store still maintains the precept upon which Henry Charles Harrod built his empire, that superior quality goods and impeccable service are more important than low prices, and as such it has become the epicentre of fashionable shopping in London.

Trafalgar Square
WEST END LONDON

Trafalgar Square is generally accepted as the very centre of the city, and it is at the heart of London culture. Here, crowds of young people gather, tourists flock to feed the pigeons, and around the square double decker buses and black taxi cabs weave an interminable path.

The idea for this large, pedestrianised square came from the architect John Nash, who designed large parts of London as we know it today, including Regent's Park and the Oxford Street layout. It was built throughout the 1830s, and shortly afterwards was crowned by the massive statue and column which stands at its centre. This monument stands over 50 metres high, and was erected to commemorate the great Lord Nelson, who was killed leading his fleet during the Battle of Trafalgar in 1805. Guarding Nelson's Column lie four immense sphinx-like bronze lions, created by Edwin Landseer.

The fountains have been a popular attraction for many years, particularly on New Year's Eve, when Trafalgar Square hosts a huge party which is attended not only by Londoners, but also by people from all over the country, drawn by the lively atmosphere and high spirits. The Square has also become a famous meeting place for all manner of rallies and demonstrations.

CASTLES &
STATELY HOMES

*The palatial homes of kings and noblemen that punctuate the English landscape
reflect the individual lifestyles and interests of these great figures. Today many of
these impressive houses are open for all to admire.*

Belvoir Castle
NEAR GRANTHAM LINCOLNSHIRE

Richard de Todeni, Standard Bearer to William the Conqueror built a typical Norman castle here in the late eleventh century. Since its original construction, Belvoir has changed hands, and been destroyed and rebuilt a number of times. It stayed in the hands of de Todeni's descendants until 1247, when it passed to Robert de Ros and his heirs, who occupied this lovely building until Lord Thomas Ros's unwise allegiance during the Wars of the Roses led to his execution. From here the castle passed to William, Lord Hastings. In his hands, the castle began to fall into ruin, under attack from supporters of de Ros.

Belvoir received a new lease of life with the ascension of Henry VII, who handed the castle back to the de Ros household, and thence, by marriage to the Earls of Rutland. It was rebuilt in typical Tudor style, abandoning the fortifications that had characterised the previous building, but it was destroyed once again by Cromwell during the English Civil War.

The Gothic-style building that now graces the countryside dates from 1816, and the castle remains in the hands of the Dukes of Rutland. It is a magnificent stately home, still bearing the marks of its long and fascinating past, including the tomb of its original owner, Richard de Todeni.

Castle Howard
NEAR HELMSLEY NORTH YORKSHIRE

Sir John Vanbrugh is generally attributed with the design of this resplendent eighteenth-century mansion, which nestles in the Howardian Hills. He came to the project with little architectural experience, however, and it is commonly assumed that his assistant Nicholas Hawksmoor had a significant influence on the construction. From the success of Castle Howard, the two men went on to work together again on the magnificent Blenheim Palace.

Commissioned by Charles Howard, the third Earl of Carlisle, the house has remained in the family since it was built, and today it houses some of the finest collections of art, furniture and porcelain in the country. It is the grounds, however, that provide the most spectacular views. Over one thousand acres surround Castle Howard, much of it carefully landscaped, with ornate fountains and neat lawns, but some parts encompass woodland and lakes. It is while exploring the grounds that the most delightful element of this area can be discovered: a peculiar abundance of old ruins including obelisks and stone towers lie scattered around the countryside. The beauty of the house and its formal gardens has captured the imaginations of many people, although its fame today stems mainly from it being used as the setting for the film *Brideshead Revisited*.

Buckingham Palace
ST JAMES'S LONDON

The London home of the British monarchy is a surprisingly unornate building lying at the head of Pall Mall in the heart of the city. Its simplicity is somehow appropriate, though, and is reflective of its importance as both a home and a symbol of Britain, where the royal family live, and where much administration takes place.

The old Buckingham House, dating from 1702, that once stood on this site was the city residence of the Duke of Buckingham, who later sold it to George III. It was converted into a palace by the architect John Nash under the commission of George IV, but the king did not live long enough to witness its completion.

Much of the present building, particularly the eastern façade facing the Mall, owes its design to the talents of Aston Webb, who recreated it just before the First World War. Today, it is perhaps the most visited sight in London, where crowds gather in the square, under the statue of Queen Victoria, to gaze at this marvellous building, to see if the royal standard is flying, indicating that the Queen is in residence, and to witness the daily Changing of the Guard, one of the country's most popular and enduring traditions.

Warwick Castle
WARWICK WARWICKSHIRE

Built under the orders of William the Conqueror, this noble castle stands on a hill on the south side of the city of Warwick, with views across the River Avon. The timber structure of the original Norman fortress was enforced by stone sometime during the twelfth century. Its intriguing mix of styles is due largely to its being rebuilt in 1694 after a fire left a trail of destruction throughout the whole city.

The beautiful gardens surrounding the castle were planned by Capability Brown in the mid-1700s, and provide over seventy acres of sculpted lawns with lovely walks, enhanced by the now-familiar peacocks which strut freely around the land. The interior of the castle is a fantastic maze of private apartments and function rooms, as well as boasting a marvellous fourteenth-century Great Hall, Guy's Tower with its unusual twelve-sided design, and Caesar's Tower, which houses the castle dungeons. It was here that prisoners from the Hundred Years War were brought and incarcerated.

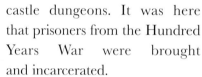

Today the castle is owned by Madame Tussaud's, who lovingly maintain this eclectic building, with its marvellous exhibitions of furniture and fittings, paintings and sculptures. It is perhaps truthfully regarded as the most beautiful medieval castle left in England.

Knebworth House
STEVENAGE HERTFORDSHIRE

Standing proudly amidst acres of park land, Knebworth House is a surprising mixture of architectural styles. It has a romantic, nineteenth-century façade, with turrets and domes, carvings and gargoyles. These were added in the mid-1800s by the novelist Sir Edward Bulwer-Lytton, who transformed the house into a fantastic Gothic building, but this fairy-tale exterior gives no indication of the great age of the house or the magnificent Tudor structure inside.

It is believed that Knebworth was originally the site of a Saxon settlement, and afterwards it lay in the hands of many famous figures, given as a reward for faithful service by Edward the Confessor and William I amongst others. It has been the home of the Lytton family for over 500 years, though, bought for the grand sum of £800 by Sir Robert Lytton in 1490.

When the Lyttons inherited Knebworth it was a simply a fifteenth-century gatehouse, which Sir Robert extended with a four-sided house and courtyard. Since this time each succeeding generation of the family has left its individual mark on the building, altering, removing and adding parts, which today make up the magnificent complexity of the present building, both inside and out.

Leeds Castle
NEAR MAIDSTONE KENT

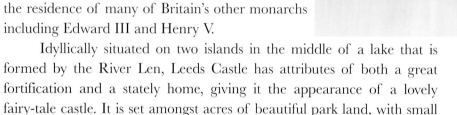

Most famously the residence of Henry VIII, the history of Leeds Castle actually extends much further back than this. A Saxon manor house stood on this spot in the ninth century, and a stone stronghold was built here by the Normans in the 1100s. In 1278, the castle was passed to the crown and Edward I and his wife Eleanor of Castile, enraptured by its outstanding setting, expanded the building, adding the impressive keep on the northern side of the castle. In its time it has been the residence of many of Britain's other monarchs including Edward III and Henry V.

Idyllically situated on two islands in the middle of a lake that is formed by the River Len, Leeds Castle has attributes of both a great fortification and a stately home, giving it the appearance of a lovely fairy-tale castle. It is set amongst acres of beautiful park land, with small

wooded areas and walkways, little bridges across meandering streams, and meadows. Inside the castle, there is an atmosphere of warmth and hospitality, far removed from the cold stone walls and dark passages that tend to characterise such castles. It is a place of noble tranquillity and serene beauty.

Palace House

BEAULIEU HAMPSHIRE

Lying serenely in a corner of the New Forest in Hampshire, the quiet village of Beaulieu was, many centuries ago, the home to one of the most famous Cistercian monasteries in England. The settlement was founded by King John in 1204, reputedly in a fit of conscience after he had ordered a group of Cistercian monks to be killed. The site grew to eventually cover nearly 10,000 acres of land, all of which was managed by the Abbey. Many people would travel here to seek sanctuary within its hallowed walls.

Like many other religious settlements, Beaulieu's prosperity did not survive Henry VIII's Dissolution of the Monasteries in the 1540s, and the Abbey was largely destroyed during this period. One part that did escape, however, was the refectory, and this magnificent and ancient building now serves as the Parish Church.

Palace House began its life as the Great Gatehouse of the original Abbey, and has now been transformed into a beautiful and majestic stately home, the seat of the Montagu family. The Montagus have had connections with the New Forest since the time of Charles II, and they still reside here in this grand building in one of England's most picturesque counties.

Chatsworth House
PEAK DISTRICT DERBYSHIRE

The first Duke of Devonshire built the majestic Chatsworth in competition with the Duke of Rutland who resided in the more understated Haddon Hall not far away. Originally an Elizabethan building, the Duke of Devonshire replaced it with the present structure at the end of the seventeenth century, and the house has remained in the family since this time.

Chatsworth was occasionally remodelled and expanded by subsequent generations of the Devonshire clan, particularly the sixth Duke, who added the magnificent north wing. Today, the building houses one of the country's most magnificent collections of art, china and furniture, collected by the family, and visitors can climb the sweeping staircases and follow the fascinating maze of rooms to admire this eclectic exhibition.

Although the house is impressive, the grounds in which it stands are unsurpassed. Designed originally in the mid-1700s by Capability Brown, they were adapted again seventy years later by Joseph Paxton. The most famous element of this garden is the Emperor Fountain, set in the middle of the lake where it still creates a magnificent and shimmering display. Surrounding this is acre upon acre of woodland, perfectly manicured lawns and flower gardens.

Haddon Hall
PEAK DISTRICT DERBYSHIRE

Two fine country houses lie just outside the town of Bakewell: Haddon Hall and Chatsworth. Haddon Hall is the older of the two, dating from medieval times. Standing gracefully on a hill above the river amongst the lush green Derbyshire countryside, it remains one of the most beautiful examples of its kind.

Originally home to the Norman Avenall household, it passed in the twelfth century to the wealthy Vernon family, who occupied the Hall for over four centuries. When Dorothy, the last heir to the Vernon inheritance, married John Manners, whose family would later become the Dukes of Rutland, they united two of the most prestigious family names in the area. Local legend states that the couple eloped together, but this is likely to be a romantic myth.

In the early 1700s the Dukes of Rutland moved their home to Belvoir Castle in Lincolnshire, leaving the magnificent Haddon Hall to crumble into ruins. It was abandoned for nearly two hundred years. At the beginning of this century, work began on restoring the Hall to its former glory, and, untouched for years, Haddon has yielded some superb finds, including paintings in the small chapel that have been hidden since the time of the Reformation.

Kenilworth Castle
KENILWORTH WARWICKSHIRE

Kenilworth Castle is largely a Norman structure, built around 1120 but with various parts added in later architectural styles. Although the castle belonged to the monarchy for many centuries, it is most famous for being the home of Robert Dudley, Earl of Leicester and his wife Amy Robsart, to whom it was granted in 1563 by Elizabeth I. The Queen made a number of visits here to see Dudley, with whom it is alleged she was having an affair. Later, when he fell out of favour with her, she had him executed, and ownership of Kenilworth later passed to a Colonel Hawkesworth, whose neglect – helped by the havoc wreaked here by Cromwell's armies – eventually caused this magnificent home to fall into ruin.

Despite this, elements of the castle's regal past are still evident. The fortifications that were added by John of Gaunt in 1170, including the Strong Tower and the Great Hall are particularly impressive. Kenilworth now hosts many events featuring plays and pageants that reflect its medieval grandeur, and the lavish entertainments that took place here during Elizabethan times.

Windsor Castle
WINDSOR BERKSHIRE

The castle at Windsor began its life as a wooden building erected by William the Conqueror after his victory at the Battle of Hastings in 1066. Since that time it has been modified and extended to become the impressive, palatial home it is today. Many of England's great monarchs have left their mark on it. The wooden building was strengthened by stone in the twelfth century by Henry II, then extended by Edward II. In 1348, Edward III founded the famous Order of the Garter here. The castle's appearance now dates mostly from the time of George IV, however, who commissioned Sir Jeffrey Wyattville to restore large parts of it.

Windsor Castle is the largest castle in Europe, and it surveys the pretty town of Windsor from its situation on the top of a steep hill. This lofty position affords fantastic views of the Berkshire countryside, and the castle itself can be observed from miles away. A notorious fire in 1992 destroyed some of the castle's most beautiful features, including St George's Hall and the Private Chapel, but happily, a careful and loving restoration has been completed.

Alnwick Castle
ALNWICK NORTHUMBERLAND

The countryside along the Northumberland shoreline is dotted with ancient relics and ruins, most notably the Norman strongholds constructed along the rocky coastline dating from the thirteenth and fourteenth centuries. Many of the towns in this area boast their own castle or fortress, making for fascinating exploration.

Alnwick is one of the finest of these castles, located on the banks of the River Aln, standing vigil today over the small market town of Alnwick, just as it has done for centuries. First built as a fortress in the eleventh century, it was strengthened and extended by the Percy family who purchased the castle in the early fourteenth century. Much of the present building owes its beauty to Salvin, the architect who redesigned it five hundred years later, and although changed, its glory has not been diminished. Inside the castle, a wealth of fine art and furniture enhance the richness of the building. Viewed from the town, Alnwick Castle looks like something out of a fairy tale, a majestic and romantic building that has been carefully preserved to maintain its original beauty.

Rochester Castle
ROCHESTER KENT

The eerie ruins of Rochester Castle survey Rochester from their vantage point on a hill above the town. The original building here was an ancient Roman fortification, which was replaced in the late eleventh century by the large stone structure – fragments of which remain today. Its most impressive feature, the keep, was completed in 1127, and was once a massive, five-storied stronghold, with walls that reach up to 12 metres thick in some parts. This was commissioned by the owner of the castle, William de Corbeuil, the Archbishop of Canterbury, and it

remained the property of the archbishops until 1215. At this time, King John instigated a siege on the castle, in an attempt to get it back from the archbishop, as his coffers were depleted. The king won the battle, but in the process, much of the building was destroyed, including one of its magnificent towers.

Today, the castle is as impressive in its ruined state as its was at the peak of its power and wealth. The broken walls and truncated stairways lend it an air of ancient mystery and fascination, and the views from the battlements across the Kent countryside give it a proud majesty and a sense of its former strength and glory.

Hampton Court Palace
EAST MOLESEY SURREY

Begun in 1514 by Thomas Wolsey, Hampton Court was not originally intended to be a palace, but rather a distinguished country residence for the Cardinal. When times began to look bad for Henry VIII's advisor, however, he offered Hampton Court to the king in the hope of getting back into the king's good books. Henry rebuilt and extended the Court, despite the fact that it already boasted over 500 rooms, and since this time, the Palace has been home to numerous kings and noblemen. The ghosts of Jane Seymour and Catherine Howard, two of Henry VIII's wives, are said to walk the halls and corridors of this majestic building to this day.

Hampton Court was redesigned by William and Mary, who commissioned the renowned architect Christopher Wren to make their changes. As such, most of the present building is an enchanting mixture of Tudor and Classical styles. The gardens are also a combination of the different tastes of these two eras. The magnificent sunken water garden and the famous maze are relics of the Tudor reign, while the formal lawns are of a later style. Changed and enhanced by other residents of Hampton Court over the years, the gardens are perhaps the most breathtaking part of the whole estate.

COUNTRY LIFE

The captivating English countryside is characterised by its rolling downs, and green valleys. The landscape is dotted with farm houses, fields full of crops and livestock, and traditional villages with picturesque cottages.

Great Tew

BANBURY OXFORDSHIRE

The town of Banbury has been immortalised in the nursery rhyme 'Ride a Cock Horse to Banbury Cross'. Although the original cross of which it tells was destroyed in the early seventeenth century, the new cross, dating from Victorian times is still a famous local landmark. It is a town dominated by marvellous medieval buildings and winding streets, enhancing the atmosphere of history and old customs.

Surrounding villages are no less charming, such as Great Tew, a picturesque little place with its own historical claims to recognition. When Viscount Falkland moved to Great Tew in 1610, and lived here until his death in 1643, his house became the meeting place of a literary circle which included Ben Johnson and Thomas Carew. Here, this group of writers would discuss not only literary matters, but also politics, religion and other important subjects. While he was living here, Falkland embarked upon his own political career, entering parliament and eventually becoming Secretary of State. He was killed in the Battle of Newbury aged only thirty-three, but he is commemorated in the village and has become its most illustrious citizen.

Main Street
CLOVELLY DEVON

Enchantingly picturesque and beautifully maintained, Clovelly has become the most famous village in Devon. This unusual little place was once a small but prosperous fishing harbour, but the herring that were the main catch in these parts are no longer as abundant as they used to be, and few people make their living from the sea here any more. Today, tourism has become the village's chief trade. Despite this, Clovelly has not succumbed to the typical commercial attractions and instead relies on its old-fashioned charm to draw the crowds.

The main street is a long and very steep winding cobbled path that leads down from the top of the village to the little harbour that nestles at the bottom, sheltered by the sheer cliff. No cars can manage the descent, and until recently the local people employed donkeys to carry goods up and down the village; today they use sledges as a means of transportation. The harbour dates back to the sixteenth century and is the central attraction in the village. A few fishing boats can still be seen here, but the view out to sea, and the simple appeal of this hidden cove is enough to make the climb back up to the village worthwhile.

Autumn on the Downs
WANTAGE OXFORDSHIRE

The village of Wantage gains its fame through being the birthplace of Alfred the Great in the ninth century AD, and it shows elements of an illustrious history since that time. A number of houses dating as far back as the fourteenth century still stand along the winding streets, and the market square which forms the hub of life in the village.

Wantage lies in the Vale of the White Horse, so called because of the immense horse carved in the chalky north slopes of the Downs.

Nobody knows the origins of this magnificent landmark, although a number of theories have been put forward, suggesting that it was intended to indicate the start of the Ridgeway, or that it represents the horse of Saint George, England's patron saint. The village is a perfect starting point for investigating the scenery of this area. In all seasons there is spectacular walking, but autumn transforms the area into a riot of fantastic colours, when the lush grassy knolls are edged with a variety of trees and shrubs in violent reds and golds. The Downs also offer a trail of marvellous relics from prehistoric times, including a fort and a number of Neolithic burial mounds.

Village Pub

EASTLEACH GLOUCESTERSHIRE

Situated at the end of the graceful Leach Valley, the village of Eastleach is one of the most attractive places in the Cotswolds. Despite its lack of the amenities and entertainments that usually draw the crowds – in fact this small pub is about the only tourist attraction there is – Eastleach remains a popular place to visit for people touring this area of the country.

The village is unusual in that it is actually divided into two parishes, one on each side of the meandering River Leach: Eastleach Turville and Eastleach Martin. Each parish has its own church, St Andrews and St Michael & St Martin, both marvellous relics of the Norman period. In the thirteenth century, the lord of the manor handed the whole village over to the administration of Gloucester Abbey.

The two parts of this village are joined by a small stone footbridge across the river, known as Keble's Bridge. John Keble, for whom it was named, was the rector of both parishes in the early nineteenth century, as well as being a poet, and, most famously, the leader of the Oxford Movement.

The Wheatsheaf

EAST HENDRED OXFORDSHIRE

This charming, snow-covered village pub lies in East Hendred, near Wantage. Its Tudor-style timber frontage is typical of the houses in the village. A typical English village, East Hendred has many thatched cottages, giving the community a traditional feel and a friendly, hospitable atmosphere.

The most notable feature of the village is its chapel. Built by monks of the Carthusian order in the thirteenth century, much of the chapel remains as it was then, with beautiful arcades and a lovely chancel. It also boasts some marvellous woodwork in the interior, including a pulpit dating from the seventeenth century and a medieval lectern. The houses that the monks once inhabited have been converted into small cottages.

The nearby Hendred Manor is the ancestral home of the Eyston family, who have owned it since the thirteenth century. They are descendants of Thomas More, and the family own many mementoes of this great historical figure. The Manor has its own chapel which dates from the same period, and is a marvellous relic of the time. All over the village evidence of the family's history in the area can be found.

Farming in the Cotswolds
NEAR BURFORD GLOUCESTERSHIRE

Although many other industries have superseded agriculture in commercial importance in England today, farming remains a significant part of English life and culture. Large expanses of the countryside are occupied by fields growing crops such as corn and wheat, or by rich green fields scattered with the slow-moving shapes of sheep or cattle. The landscape is divided by hedgerows, fences and drystone walls into neat patterns of fields and meadows, broken occasionally by the farm buildings. One of the most enduringly picturesque sights in England is that of haystacks neatly piled up in the fields after the harvest – another celebration of tradition.

The farmland pictured here lies on the border of Gloucestershire, near Burford, an alluring little town set on the meandering course of the River Windrush. The nutritious pastures of the Cotswold Hills make good grazing for sheep, and this has created a significant industry of wool-trading in this part of the country. Burford is one of the main trading centres for wool, although, like so many other Cotswold towns, it also relies heavily on the tourist trade.

Village Green
CAVENDISH SUFFOLK

A typical Suffolk village, Cavendish is dominated by pretty thatched cottages around the village green. Their clean, pastel pink painted exteriors add an unusual charm to the place which is also characterised by a number of older buildings. The most beautiful of these is the village church, with its lovely fourteenth-century tower. Inside the church is some exquisite panelling, and a clerestory constructed of flint. It also contains the tombs of the Cavendish family, the old Lords of the Manor.

On the outskirts of the village lies Cavendish Hall, a magnificent early nineteenth-century structure of Classical architecture. The Old Rectory, once belonging to the church, is now owned by Sue Ryder, who has helped refugees from all over the world. The village also has a museum and gallery, which are housed in the nearby Nether Hall, which dates from the fifteenth century.

This abundance of architecture and history from different eras makes Cavendish a fascinating and unusual village. Despite these attractions, it retains its peaceful atmosphere, traditional village demeanour and gentle way of life.

The Manor House
LOWER BROCKHAMPTON
HEREFORD & WORCESTERSHIRE

Lower Brockhampton lies not far from the village of Brockhampton in Brockhampton Park. Here, the captivating little manor house stands on an island surrounded by a moat. This delightful two-storied timber structure, which can still be visited, was built towards the end of the fourteenth century, and is remarkable in that parts of it have remained essentially unchanged since it was constructed. These include the finest feature of the house: the great hall with its lovely galleries.

In front of the manor house stands the diminutive gatehouse, which dates from the fifteenth century. Erected in the same style as the main building, with two storeys and a timber frame, this striking addition is a perfect complement to the beauty of the manor and the peaceful little moat.

Not far from this spot stand the ruins of the old Norman chapel that would once have served the manor house. This has been sadly neglected since the church was moved in 1798, but its remains are a pleasant sight on the landscape in this hidden corner of the county.

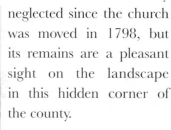

Whitchurch
NEAR READING BERKSHIRE

The town of Reading lies at the convergence of the rivers Thames and Kennet – a situation that has afforded it much commercial prosperity. The town expanded from an original ninth-century Danish settlement, which made use of the plentiful water supply, and flourished for many centuries. It became the home of a Benedictine Abbey in the early twelfth century, established by the king at the time, Henry I. This successful little community was granted its first charter in 1253. By the twentieth century it had grown into an important centre for the manufacture of machinery, and is the heart of the county's agricultural administration.

This exquisite view of a fairy tale hamlet lies not far from the town of Reading. The green shrubs and trees in the foreground of the picture here stand on the banks of a backwater of the Thames. The brilliant terracotta colour of the houses reflects in the blue of the gently undulating water. An air of stillness hangs over the village, with its neat tended lawns stretching down to the river banks. It is a scene that epitomises England at its most beautiful and colourful.

Hedge Laying
APPLETON OXFORDSHIRE

The hedgerows of England are a sadly under-rated part of the landscape, despite the fact that they are one of the country's oldest landmarks and many of them have been standing for centuries. In many parts of the country these ancient shrubs suffer from neglect, growing wild and abandoned or simply being destroyed. Nowadays, however, increasing efforts are being made to preserve them, by rebuilding and careful tending. In rural areas, too, new hedges are being planted, and here the process of establishing these natural borders can be seen.

The tiny village of Appleton, near where this picture was taken, is a typical Oxfordshire village, situated a short way from Stanton Harcourt, with its fifteenth-century manor house. The poet Alexander Pope stayed at Stanton while working on his translation of Homer's *Iliad* in the eighteenth century. Appleton itself has its own manor house dating from the late twelfth century, a regal addition to this little village. Not far away, the River Windrush winds along the countryside through many equally lovely places.

Combine Harvest Scene
HARWELL OXFORDSHIRE

The importance of farming in this area of the country is demonstrated here, by this typical scene of English rural life. Combine harvesters are a familiar sight in the fields and on the Downs, where ripe crops abound at the end of the summer months. The golden colour of the crops complementing the pale blue of the late summer sky is a familiar sight. Farming was not always as straightforward as it is in the twentieth century, and for hundreds of years, the people of England would scratch out a living with the most primitive of tools. Often they would work for a landlord, who demanded hard labour for little reward. Payment frequently came in the form of food and housing, or if financial reward for their work was offered, the labourers would often receive only a small percentage of it.

New developments in mechanisation, particularly in the Industrial Revolution, meant an end to such hard toil for ever. Today, these giant machines save time, money and energy: a symbol of modern life on an unchanged landscape.

The Village Pond
FINCHINGFIELD ESSEX

Finchingfield is a traditional Essex village: a group of clean, whitewashed houses situated around a duckpond and a green. The remaining village buildings are scattered around according to no particular plan, but this only adds to the charm of this enchanting place. These buildings include an unusual windmill, painted green, which surveys the village from a short distance away. Next to the windmill is a bizarre structure known as the Round House, a cottage built in a hexagonal shape in the eighteenth century by the local Lords of the Manor from Spains Hall.

The Hall itself is a fine building of red brick on the outskirts of Finchingfield, its unplanned and random structure an appropriate reflection of the eccentric characters who have lived here in the past. In the seventeenth century, the Hall was owned by William Kempe, who honoured a vow of silence he inflicted upon himself after he had wrongly accused his wife of adultery. During the seven years he was not speaking, he filled his time by digging ponds in the acres of land that surrounded Spains Hall. The large lake that lies in the grounds today is made up of eight of these original ponds.

Typical Cotswold Street
BROADWAY HEREFORD & WORCESTERSHIRE

Situated on the edge of the Cotswolds, Broadway is one of the most popular villages for visitors to begin an exploration of the area. The village, unsurprisingly, takes its name from its wide streets. Many years ago, before the settlement grew to its present size, there were two streams running down the sides of the old street, which were eventually covered over, greatly expanding the width of the road.

The buildings in the village date from as far back as Elizabethan times, and the main street in Broadway contains some fine and fascinating structures. The most interesting of these is the Lygon Arms. In times past this was a manor house and it numbers Charles I amongst its many famous residents.

Standing vigil from its position on a hill above the village is the Broadway Tower. This was built in the eighteenth century, and gains much of its fame from being a popular retreat for artists of the Pre-Raphaelite movement, in particular William Morris. For centuries before the Tower was built, this was an ancient beacon site, and from here the views out across the country are truly astounding: on a clear day, the horizon encompasses a dozen counties.

CITIES
& TOWNS

The built-up areas of England range from quiet market towns hiding secrets of an illustrious past, to thriving industrial cities. Each one exhibits an individuality and character created by its history and inhabitants.

Oxford High Street
OXFORD OXFORDSHIRE

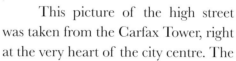

Set amidst the grand surroundings of ancient buildings within verdant countryside, the centre of Oxford thrives today as it has for many centuries. The lovely cobbled streets are lined with shops that range from the usual high street chain stores to tiny exclusive boutiques. Unsurprising for a city that has been England's main seat of learning for hundreds of years, there are also numerous bookshops: new, second-hand and antique. These can be found not only along the main streets, but also lining the maze of passageways and alleys that weave a complex path away from the bustle of the centre to the tranquil outskirts of the city.

This picture of the high street was taken from the Carfax Tower, right at the very heart of the city centre. The name Carfax derives from the Latin term *quadrifurua*, meaning 'four-forked'. From this point, the four main streets stretch out in opposing directions: to the North, South, East and West. The Tower was built on the spot which marked the centre of the town in the medieval era. At this time, there were walls running along the outskirts marking the city's boundaries.

Piccadilly Circus
WEST END LONDON

Piccadilly Circus is one of the most popular areas of central London today. Bright, lively and packed with bars, restaurants, shops and theatres, it is a hub of London's shopping fraternity during the day, and still draws crowds of Londoners and tourists to its neon-lit, open-all-hours entertainments after dark.

The circus was originally part of the designs drawn up by the architect John Nash when he was commissioned to plan the Regent's Park area at the turn of the nineteenth century, and it lies at the junction of Regent Street and Shaftesbury Avenue in the heart of the West End. Piccadilly has altered immensely since Nash's first vision of it, but despite its obvious commercial flavour, it cannot completely hide its nineteenth-century origins, particularly with buildings like the London Pavilion, erected in 1885, and home to Music Hall entertainments – the Victorian equivalent of the nightclubs and bars that dominate the area now.

The best-known of all Piccadilly Circus's features, however, is Gilbert-Scott's Statue of Eros. This was unveiled in 1892, a memorial to the Victorian phil-anthropist, the Earl of Shaftesbury. Contrary to popular opinion, the aluminium figure it displays is not Eros at all, but an Angel of Charity.

Beach and Pier
SANDOWN ISLE OF WIGHT

The Isle of Wight was taken over with little resistance by the mighty Romans in AD 43, and in later centuries dominance of the island fell to the Jutes and the Danes. It remained relatively undisturbed, however, until Regency times, and increased in popularity with the English aristocracy when Queen Victoria transferred her seaside residence from Brighton to Osborne House here on the island.

Together, Sandown and Shanklin form the largest seafront resort on the Isle of Wight, and the crux of its tourist trade. These busy strips of beach draw crowds from mainland England and abroad to enjoy the warm climate and many attractions, both natural and man-made that the area has to offer. The main feature along the sand at Sandown is the pier, which is the only pleasure pier that is still used on the island.

The scenery around the areas of Sandown and Shanklin have only served to enhance its popularity. The beautiful strips of sand are set against a backdrop of dramatic cliffs and grassy coastal paths with marvellous views out across the sea. Inland, away from the bustle of the town centres there are still many places that seem unexplored and wildly remote, despite the island's small size.

Petersgate

YORK NORTH YORKSHIRE

In ecclesiastical terms, York is the centre of Anglican worship and administration. The large number of churches and other religious buildings that were situated here by the sixteenth century were badly affected by Henry VIII's endorsement of the Protestant cause and the subsequent Dissolution of the Monasteries. Traces of the town's significant religious past, however, can still be seen, not only in the marvellous religious buildings that remain, but in many of the customs and traditions that abound in this area. One of the most fascinating of these traditions is the York Mystery Plays, a cycle of plays performed in York at four year intervals. They originated in the fourteenth century, and chart the creation, fall and redemption of Man.

York also has strong industrial links. In the nineteenth century during the Industrial Revolution, it ranked second only to London in importance and as major trading city. Today it remains at the heart of Yorkshire's commercial success. The city centre is a hive of activity all year round, with parades of shops along main streets and winding medieval alleyways, providing a pleasant combination of the ancient and the contemporary.

Covent Garden Market
WEST END LONDON

Covent Garden derives its name from the convent garden that used to exist here, and which supplied produce to Westminster Abbey. The present layout of the area, influenced by the Italian piazza style, was designed by Inigo Jones in 1631, who intended the Garden to be a desirable, fashionable part of the city. His plan was soon to be thwarted, however, as market stalls sprang up to sell produce to the wealthy people who lived there. As these expanded, the tone of the neighbourhood fell: brothels and gambling dens thrived and the whole area became an unhealthy mixture of rotting market foodstuffs and wild behaviour.

In the nineteenth century, Charles Fowler designed the covered market that forms the central part of Covent Garden today. A unique building, characterised by its glass roof and iron framework, it marked the beginning in a revival of fortunes for the area. Although the original market moved away from Covent Garden in the 1970s, a new generation of stall-holders now occupy the market both inside and out, selling gifts and crafts. It has also become one of the most popular haunts for Londoners, with a host of bars, pubs and restaurants. Street entertainers like this are an everyday sight at Covent Garden, adding colour and interest to this lively place.

Regency Terraced Houses
LEAMINGTON SPA WARWICKSHIRE

Like most other spa towns in England, Leamington's heyday dates from Regency and Victorian times, when the fashion for spending a few weeks every year indulging in the healing properties of the mineral springs was at its height amongst the upper classes in England. The houses pictured here are typical examples of Leamington's architectural heritage. Dating from the Regency period, their clean white façades and impressively uniform structure are characteristic of the time. The houses run in a gentle arc, with green lawns at the front. In many ways, these are reminiscent of the residences that can be found in England's greatest spa town, Bath, with its particularly beautiful Royal Crescent.

Today, Leamington retains its air of opulence, despite the decline in economy that the waning of the trend for taking the waters brought with it. It is now characterised by a small but busy town centre remarkable for its antique shops. Its sense of gentility still attracts the tourists who come to revel in the area's rich past.

Church Street

WINDSOR BERKSHIRE

Characterised by enchanting cobbled streets running up and down the hills, and dominated by the imposing castle standing at the pinnacle of one of these, Windsor is a charming, but busy town, that manages to maintain a village atmosphere. This is owed in part to its medieval history, which is evident in many of the traditional half-timbered houses that line the small streets, some of which have been converted into shops or pubs.

As the home to England's kings and queens for over 900 years, Windsor has an undeniable air of grandeur. This distinguished air is further enhanced by the town's close proximity to Windsor Great Park, a vast expanse of green lawns and woodland that provides peaceful walks and beautiful scenery. The town of Windsor that is so popular today, however, is New Windsor. The original city was founded a few miles away, and was the seat of the Saxon kings of England: it is here that archaeologists have discovered the relics of a building believed to be the ancient palace of Edward the Confessor.

The Eastgate Clock
CHESTER CHESHIRE

The city of Chester grew from a Roman settlement on the River Dee, and has had a long and turbulent history. Occupied by the Vikings and the Scots, who did it much damage, the town was eventually rebuilt and expanded by Aethelflaed, Alfred the Great's daughter, only to suffer again after the Norman conquest. It became a thriving port from the twelfth century, and this new prosperity lasted for over 200 years, until the harbour began to silt up. Today, however, Chester is a thriving city once more, a city that has retained its charm and flaunts its fascinating history in many ways.

The city walls largely follow those of the ancient Roman settlement, and they are dominated by the four splendid city gates, which were rebuilt in a fine style in the eighteenth and nineteenth centuries. Close to the Eastgate lies one of Chester's most famous landmarks – the Eastgate Clock. This was designed by the architect John Douglas, and made by J. B. Joyce of Whitchurch. The clock, with its magnificent wrought-iron surround and distinctive face, was presented to the city to mark Queen Victoria's Diamond Jubilee in 1897.

Blackpool Tower
BLACKPOOL LANCASHIRE

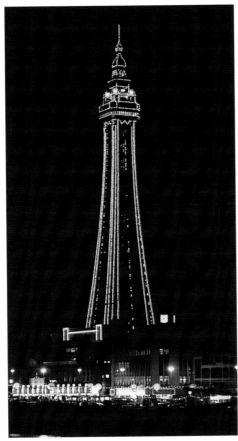

Blackpool is one of the most famous seaside resorts in England. Along the seafront runs the Golden Mile, a stretch of beach that is characterised by a large number of bright amusement arcades, fairground rides, bingo halls and theatres. It also boasts three piers, which date from the nineteenth century.

The most dominant landmark along this stretch, however, is the dazzling Blackpool Tower. Built in 1894, this incredible 158-metre structure was based on the Eiffel Tower in Paris. Inside, its floors are full of typical seaside entertainments, including the tower's own circus and an amazing ballroom, with music provided by a grand Wurlitzer organ. The Tower has naturally suffered over the years due to its popularity, but recent work has restored it to its former Victorian glory.

The Blackpool Tower forms just part of the famous Blackpool Illuminations, when, for two months of the year, the town is lit up by myriad bulbs, creating a magnificent spectacle. The Illuminations use a total of over half a million bulbs, and people flock from all over the country to see the colourful carnival-style lights.

Albert Dock
LIVERPOOL MERSEYSIDE

The port at Liverpool was built under the orders of King John in the early thirteenth century, but it was not until the 1800s that it really began to flourish. At one time Chester was the main sea port in England, but when the harbour there began to silt up, Liverpool's prime location meant that it soon took over much of the old port's trade and industry. When the first dock with locks opened in 1715, it virtually guaranteed the city's future success and prosperity.

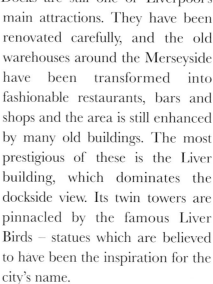

Albert Dock, opened by Prince Albert in 1846, was the first dock to be constructed using bricks and metal, abandoning the traditional material of wood that had proved so susceptible to fire in the past. Sadly they ceased to be fully functioning docks in 1972. Although the city is no longer the main centre of maritime industry in England, the Docks are still one of Liverpool's main attractions. They have been renovated carefully, and the old warehouses around the Merseyside have been transformed into fashionable restaurants, bars and shops and the area is still enhanced by many old buildings. The most prestigious of these is the Liver building, which dominates the dockside view. Its twin towers are pinnacled by the famous Liver Birds – statues which are believed to have been the inspiration for the city's name.

Portsmouth Dockyard
PORTSMOUTH HAMPSHIRE

For centuries, Portsmouth has enjoyed the prestige of being England's most important seafaring town. The first port was established here in Norman times, but it did not begin to grow until Henry VII made this the royal dockyard, and the centre of naval activity in the country. Its ideal situation on a peninsula which forms a large natural harbour has meant that no other port town in England has been able to compete with its convenience and size.

The Dockyard remains Portsmouth's most popular and fascinating feature. It is home to some of the most famous ships in England's naval history. The first armoured battleship to grace the waters, the *HMS Warrior* is on show here. First launched in 1860, the *Warrior* was the most advanced warship of its time, and was thought to be virtually indestructible. Its designers never had the satisfaction of proving this, though as, ironically, the *Warrior* never participated in active service. The other two main attractions here are Nelson's flagship, the *HMS Victory*, and the *Mary Rose*, which was shipwrecked off the coast in the sixteenth century, and lay undisturbed on the sea floor for four hundred years until it was exhumed recently, and carefully restored to become one of the great prides of Portsmouth.

Montpellier Gardens
HARROGATE NORTH YORKSHIRE

Once one of the north's most illustrious spa towns, Harrogate today relies on the tourist trade to maintain its commercial success. Despite this, however, it remains relatively unspoilt, and careful preservation and maintenance of its many beautiful lawns and gardens such as this, ensure a neat and noble aspect that reflects the history of the town.

Like most of England's spa towns, Harrogate's popularity was not to rise until Edwardian and Victorian times, despite the fact that the springs were discovered in the sixteenth century. Here, the waters are rich in iron and sulphur, and wealthy Londoners, including royalty, would travel here to improve their health. Harrogate's period of affluence was relatively short, and its popularity began to wane after the First World War, never to achieve quite the same status again. Today it is a renowned and busy shopping centre with an abundance of antique shops and exclusive little boutiques. It is also known for its lovely gardens and park land, of which The Spray, reputedly the largest lawn in the world, is one.

Northumberland Passage

BATH AVON

The busy shopping area of Bath boasts an abundance of great architecture, which spans the centuries from Roman times to its great period of prosperity in the Georgian and Victorian eras. Everywhere one turns in the city, one is greeted with the breathtaking buildings that reflect the city's illustrious history. Despite the vast array of shops, restaurants, pubs and bars, Bath has managed to retain its ancient dignity.

The whole area is endowed with a stately air that derives from the careful planning of the street layouts and the pleasant harmony of the golden bricks used in its architecture. Its regal yet fashionable air dates back to the time of the infamous Beau Nash, who was made Master of the Ceremonies in Regency Bath. This time of opulence and splendour was characterised by balls, parties and other lavish entertainments, which Nash encouraged in an unprecedented way. An incurable gambler himself, Nash encouraged the vice in the city, and in so doing amassed a vast fortune. He instigated a number of new laws and reforms, some of which were well-intentioned,some selfish, and others downright bizarre. Today he is looked upon as Bath's most notorious and loveable citizen.

Big Ben
WESTMINSTER LONDON

It is generally assumed that the name Big Ben refers to the clock tower that stands impressively over the Houses of Parliament in Westminster. In fact it is the name of the massive 14-tonne bell inside the tower that rings out the hour across the city of London. The bell was installed in 1858, and was named after the Chief Commissioner of Works at that time, Sir Benjamin Hall.

The clock itself is the largest in Great Britain, its four faces, made of hollow copper, have been the definitive timekeeping mechanism in the country for over 100 years, and crowds of people flock here every day to see it. The tower that houses the clock is a beautifully ornate piece of architecture, and it stands majestically together with the Houses of Parliament on the banks of the Thames. It is at night, however, that one gains the best view of Big Ben's public face. The clock is lit up and a flood of golden light shines over the tower and the Parliament buildings. It has become a familiar landmark in the city, and an enduring symbol of London.

QEII Ocean Liner
SOUTHAMPTON HAMPSHIRE

The large, industrial city of Southampton lays claim to being one of England's most vital ports, second only to Portsmouth in importance. Set in the natural harbour formed by the River Test and the River Itchen, Southampton is no longer the central docking port for the massive steam liners that used to dominate its waters, but it is still a thriving and – despite its size – lovely city, with numerous reminders of its ancient history, including long stretches of the city walls, erected in medieval times.

The Romans were the first to make use of Southampton's ideal setting, and since these times, the port has seen many great figures embark on journeys that were to shape the history not only of England, but of the whole world. From here the Pilgrim Fathers set off in the *Mayflower* in 1620, Henry V left for France to embark on a series of battles that were to culminate in the infamous Battle of Agincourt, and the *Titanic* began its first and only journey. Until the 1930s, Southampton was the main departure point for the huge passenger steam ships that crossed the Atlantic, and today, cruise ships such as the famous *QEII* are still a familiar site docked here in Southampton.

THE MAGIC OF ENGLAND

The enchantment of this country can be seen at every turn. The colours of the changing seasons, the unsurpassed beauty of its villages, the regal parks and gardens, and the spirit of its people all combine to make up the unique country that is England.

Burnham Beeches
NEAR EGYPT BUCKINGHAMSHIRE

The beech tree is native to England, and it has been part of the English landscape for over six thousand years, thriving in the damp climate. It is surprising, however, that many of the beechwood forests that characterise certain parts of England such as the New Forest and the Forest of Dean are not natural, but man-made, planted on the site of ancient oak forests.

It became fashionable in the eighteenth century to plant beeches in the grounds of country houses, and in small groups on hillsides to provide wooded glades for the enjoyment of the wealthy. Burnham Beeches is one of these contrived – but nonetheless beautiful – areas of beechwood forest. Situated not far from Maidenhead, Burnham was bought by the City of London Corporation in 1879. It was intended as a refuge for Londoners wishing to escape the smoke of the city. The forest now spans over 400 acres and is home to many wild animals, birds and plant life. Although the beeches here are smaller than those found elsewhere in England due to the acidity of the soil in which they grow, the forest is still an enchanting and impressive place to visit.

Imperial Gardens
CHELTENHAM GLOUCESTERSHIRE

Cheltenham was for many centuries just another small town in the Cotswolds with nothing in particular to distinguish it. When a spring was found here in 1716, however, the discovery changed the fortunes of the town forever. Although the boom for spa towns did not happen until later in the century, Cheltenham slowly began to attract more attention, and when George III visited here in 1788, the town knew it had made a name for itself. The mass of architecture dating from this period is an indication of the town's commercial success at the time. Later on, Cheltenham became a popular place for old soldiers, who came to be near the healing spring waters and to retire. Today the town retains much of its old dignity and splendour.

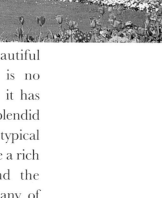

Possibly the most beautiful Cotswold town, Cheltenham is no longer a central spa town, but it has many other attractions. Its splendid buildings, characterised by the typical golden grey Cotswold stone have a rich and magic feel to them, and the carefully planned gardens – many of them laid out at the time of the town's original prosperity – provide a fantastic spectacle in the summer when they are bursting with colour and warmth.

Windpump
THURNE DYKE NORFOLK

Sights like this one are common along the banks of the rivers that flow through the attractive Norfolk Broads. Wind and water pumps stand picturesquely along the routes of the Yare, the Thurne and the Bure. Many are now derelict, but others have been preserved, and all serve as a reminder of a time when the natural elements of wind and water were harnessed as essential means for industry and they were the centre of local activity.

The windpump here at Thurne Dyke was neglected after it ceased to run, but it has now been restored, and its lovely white-painted exterior and soaring sails stand out against the skyline to a dramatic effect. The interior of the pump now houses an exhibition illustrating how such devices worked, and visitors can climb up the ladder to the top of the mill.

By far the best way to appreciate the beauty of these old buildings, and indeed the surrounding countryside is from the rivers themselves. Boat trips through the broads have long been extremely popular. In the past this has created significant problems as the banks were being worn away by the continual wash created by boats passing up- and down-river, but since the area has been designated a National Park, efforts have been made to stem this erosion.

Bluebells
CHRISTMAS COMMON BUCKINGHAMSHIRE

This dazzling carpet of bluebells is in the woodland of Christmas Common which lies on the boundary between the counties of Oxfordshire and Buckinghamshire. It is not known exactly why Christmas Common is called this, but one theory suggests that it derives from the many holly trees which have flourished here for centuries. Before the rise in popularity of the traditional fir tree as the symbol of Christmas in England, holly was often used for the same purpose. Another suggestion is that it gains its name from the celebrations that occurred after a temporary truce was called at Christmas between the Cavaliers and the Roundheads during the notorious Civil War. Whatever the origins of the name, however, it is an appropriately festive title for this scenic area.

In the spring, one of the greatest pleasures nature has to offer is the unexpected sight of a carpet of bluebells like these growing in woodland glades all over the English countryside. Here they provide a breathtaking blanket of vivid purple and blue, hiding the dull brown of the earth beneath.

Winter Scene
ARDINGTON OXFORDSHIRE

The village of Ardington is situated a short distance from Wantage, the birthplace of Alfred the Great. Pictured here on a bright, snowy winter morning, Ardington possesses the charm and magic that characterises so many small villages around England. An air of stillness and peace pervades it, enhanced by the blanket of snow. The manor of Ardington had its centre at Ardington House, a short distance from the village. This elegant country home was erected in the early part of the eighteenth century and was once owned by the area's most illustrious citizen, Lord Wantage.

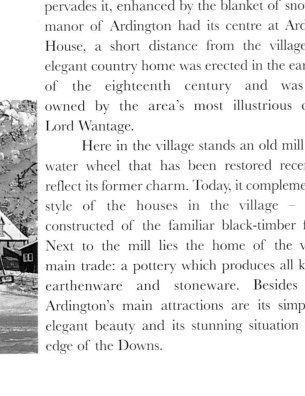

Here in the village stands an old mill with a water wheel that has been restored recently to reflect its former charm. Today, it complements the style of the houses in the village – mostly constructed of the familiar black-timber frames. Next to the mill lies the home of the village's main trade: a pottery which produces all kinds of earthenware and stoneware. Besides these, Ardington's main attractions are its simple and elegant beauty and its stunning situation on the edge of the Downs.

Daffodils at Waddesdon Manor
AYLESBURY BUCKINGHAMSHIRE

This breathtaking display of daffodils is part of the marvellous gardens at Waddesdon Manor in Aylesbury. The Manor is an elegant structure built in 1874 in the style of a French chateau for Baron Ferdinand de Rothschild. The furniture and fittings inside the house all accurately reflect eighteenth-century France, and include a fine array of wooden panelling that was acquired from houses in France. It is the collection of art, however, that is the Manor's greatest asset. The works of artists such as Gainsborough and Rubens are on display here, along with a variety of Old Masters.

The grounds of the house were designed by Laine, and comprise incredible sweeping lawns and park land. This field of daffodils is one of its finest features. Daffodils are a common sight in England, and their welcome appearance heralds the arrival of Spring. Their vivid colour and beautiful shape evoke a typically English image, and the flowers have been the inspiration of poets and painters for centuries. They flourish in March and April, and are often seen growing wild in woods and fields. The daffodil has become an integral part of the English countryside.

Sunset
LONGWORTH OXFORDSHIRE

As the sun sets over the Oxfordshire countryside, a picture-perfect scene of warm tranquillity pervades the landscape. This view is a typical one at dusk all over England. The wide fields spread out to the horizon, with a few scattered trees silhouetted against the glorious colours of the evening, and the low clouds, which are characteristic of the country.

The village of Longworth, where this photograph was taken, is a tiny but bewitching place. Its one claim to distinction is that the writer R. D. Blackmore was born here. Apart from this, its picturesque aspect and beautiful surrounding countryside make it a spell-binding spot to visit. Around this part of Oxfordshire, there are many tiny villages like Longworth, tucked away among the fields and hills. Tributaries of the Thames and the River Windrush flow through this area and around the countryside, and on the outskirts of these villages, small stone bridges cross the streams and rivulets that serve these rivers, adding to the endearing aspect of this most lovely area.

Swans
SANDFORD LOCK OXFORDSHIRE

Sandford Lock is situated on the Thames not far from Oxford. Sandford is a peaceful hamlet, a far cry from the lively city just beyond it. From the village, a small winding pathway leads down to the river and the lock. The lock is the second on the Thames down-river from Oxford, and is home to many wild birds like these swans that make their nests along the banks of the river. The riverbanks here are dominated by chestnut trees making this part of the Thames placid and peaceful.

It is not unusual to discover places like Sandford in close proximity to big cities. That modern development does not always encroach upon the beauty of the small undisturbed areas around them is part of England's charm, and as a consequence England has a large number of villages like this, with an air of old-fashioned peacefulness, as though the place and the people have not changed since the hamlets first grew up around the rivers and in the remote parts of the countryside. Although not far away in Oxford, the river teems with rowers and punters from the university colleges, this section of the water is free from such traffic.

Jephson Gardens
LEAMINGTON SPA WARWICKSHIRE

Leamington, a spa town, owes its current popularity and prosperity to the Victorian fashion for 'taking the waters'. Although the mineral-rich springs have been here for many centuries, it was not until the end of the eighteenth century that people first began to take an interest in the healing powers of the waters that gushed up from deep within the ground. The first bath was opened here in 1786, and Leamington has enjoyed certain popularity since that time.

The town's charm lies in its impressive buildings, dating from Regency and Victorian times, and the lovely manicured gardens that were designed to enhance the calming atmosphere of the place. The Jephson Gardens are some of the most beautiful in this area. They lie in front of the old Pump Room, and were named after one of Leamington's most eminent citizens Dr Henry Jephson, who was the town's physician. The Gardens are carefully maintained, and in the summer they provide a riot of beauty and colour to complement the majestic buildings that lie all around, in an apt reflection of Leamington's former days of grandeur.

Ashridge Forest
NEAR TRING HERTFORDSHIRE

The beautiful Ashridge Forest – resplendent here in its autumnal glory – lies on the edge of the small town of Tring. The mansion house that shares its name is a looming gothic-inspired edifice dating from the early nineteenth century. It was built on the site of the ancient monastery of Bonhommes, which was established in 1283. Local tales would have one believe that this monastery had in its possession the most marvellous religious relic of all: a drop of the blood of Christ shed at the Crucifixion. Later on, this was the place where, in the sixteenth century, Mary, the Queen of England had her sister Elizabeth arrested. The mysterious atmosphere of the site spreads to the sur-rounding area to include the small forest, which is a magical place, boasting magnificent trees and fascinating wildlife.

The old town of Tring, nestling at the foot of the Chiltern Hills, is very much associated with the name of Rothschild, the local landlords, whose seat was based here at Tring Park. One of the most significant legacies of this family is the Zoological Museum in the town, which was established by the second Lord Rothschild.

The George
DORCHESTER-ON-THAMES OXFORDSHIRE

The village of Dorchester lies on the Thames, and is typified by its black and white timbered houses and its lovely pubs and inns, like the one pictured here. The quiet tranquil atmosphere that hangs over the town today, however, belies a long and full history.

The remains of a Roman fort stand silently on a hillside nearby known as Wittenham Clumps. From here, the soldiers would have been able to keep a careful look out over the surrounding hills and fields, and the stretch of the Thames that passes through it, watching for any approaching danger. Remnants of a rampart also dating from Roman times are evident in the town, too, and the countryside that stretches out for miles around provided large numbers of intriguing ancient sites, including a fortified town and stones dating from Neolithic times.

The old-fashioned coach parked at the front of the inn in this picture is also an appropriate symbol of the town's history. At one time, this was an important staging post on the road from London to Oxford, where weary travellers would alight for refreshment, and possibly a room for the night.

Torquay Harbour
TORQUAY DEVON

Torquay, Paignton and Brixham have been christened, unofficially, the 'English Riviera'. The area's warm climate and lush vegetation have made it an extremely popular holiday destination in England. Once a small village, with fishing as its main trade and industry, Torquay has grown into a bustling and lively town. Its prosperity dates from the middle of the nineteenth century, when the climate and sea air became a fashionable attraction for wealthy invalids. The poet Elizabeth Barrett Browning, who suffered from lifelong ill health, spent three years here.

Life in Torquay is still very much centred around its charming harbour. The tranquillity found here is unusual for such a thriving town. The small yachts and other sea craft that lie moored here on the gently swelling waters make for a pleasantly picturesque scene. Along the edge of the harbour, pristine white hotels and restaurants add to the pleasant scene, and at night, the harbour is lit by the lights from the surrounding buildings, which reflect and dance in the water, giving this essentially English resort a warm Mediterranean atmosphere and a magical quality.

Roses on a Cottage Wall
LYNDHURST HAMPSHIRE

The combination of a thatched cottage and its climbing rose bush is a perfectly typical English village scene, and is one that can be found all over the country. Lyndhurst, particularly, enjoys many such examples of enchanting rural England. The village is the unofficial capital of the New Forest, and it is certainly one of the best places to start exploring this marvellous area.

The New Forest was created in 1079, and was intended as a hunting park for Norman noblemen and royalty. Since this time, it has been carefully preserved to maintain its setting of ancient, undisturbed tranquillity. Situated between the large cities of Southampton and Bournemouth, the New Forest is surprisingly remote and undeveloped. Lyndhurst has its own claims to historical beauty, largely the village church, which is characterised by a Pre-Raphaelite luminescence and opulence. The two main windows are the work of Edward Burne-Jones, one of the most influential designers in William Morris's company, which created textiles, tapestries and stained glass. Also dominating the small church is a fresco painted by Lord Leighton, depicting the Wise and Foolish Virgins. This rich artistic heritage, together with its charming cottages and beautiful setting, has made Lyndhurst a most popular spot for visitors to the New Forest.

Gold Hill

SHAFTESBURY DORSET

The village of Shaftesbury stands on the pinnacle of a steep hill, from which the surrounding countryside can be surveyed in all its rich grandeur. The village boasts a proud history, starting in AD 880 when a settlement for Benedictine nuns was founded here. A century later, the bones of Edward the Martyr were brought to the Abbey here, and in their wake came flocks of pilgrims. Little of the Abbey survives today, but the ruins are a haunting testimony to the area's past. The village grew and prospered, and although relics of its medieval heyday are rare now, a few can still be seen. The best-preserved of these is St Peter's Church which stands on the edge of the old market square. St Peter's is just one of many churches that were to be found in the village and its surrounding area. At one time, there was even a castle here, although this has since been razed to the ground.

Gold Hill is an enchanting cobbled pathway leading down from the village. It affords some of the best views that the village has to offer. The countryside for miles around can be surveyed from the top of the hill. Surrounded by fields and streams, farmland and woods, the village of Shaftesbury is the epitome of a typical English village.

England Past and Present

This map of England and Wales was drawn up in 1579 by the cartographer Christopher Saxon. During the Anglo-Saxon era, England was divided into seven kingdoms – East Anglia, Wessex, Sussex, Essex, Kent, Mercia and Northumbria. Since the sixteenth century, when this map was created, the counties in England have shifted and merged. Many still retain their names and borders, while others have changed their boundaries whilst retaining their names. Detailed below are the modern counties with their sixteenth-century equivalents. These are followed by the page numbers on which locations are featured in this book.

Avon *(Somersetus)*
21, 52, 53, 55, 67, 97, 175

Berkshire *(Berceria)*
104, 112, 115, 140, 155, 169

Buckinghamshire *(Buckinghamia)*
35, 71, 74, 184, 180, 186

Cambridgeshire *(Cantabrigia)*
57, 63, 75,

Cheshire *(Cestria)*
72, 170

Cornwall *(Cornubia)*
32, 36, 47

Cumbria *(Cumbria)*
46, 76, 87

Derbyshire *(Derbia)*
38, 73, 78, 83, 136, 137

Devon *(Devonia)*
34, 45, 148, 192

Dorset *(Dorcestria)*
40, 85, 117, 120, 194

Durham *(Dunelmesis epis)*
28

East Sussex *(Southsexia)*
37, 58, 123

Essex *(Essexia)*
158

Gloucestershire *(Gloucestria)*
27, 42, 65, 80, 86, 150, 152, 182

Hampshire *(Southamptonia)*
19, 96, 135, 173, 177, 193

Hereford and Worcester
(Herefordia & Wigornia)
26, 121, 154, 159

Hertfordshire *(Hartfordia)*
102, 133, 190

Humberside *(Eboracum)*
118

Isle of Wight
(Southamptonia)
114, 122, 165

Kent *(Cantium)*
14, 134, 142

Lancashire *(Lancastria)*
171

Lincolnshire *(Lincolnia)*
16, 128

London *(Middlesexia)*
20, 50, 62, 66, 94, 105, 119, 124, 125,
131, 164, 167, 176

Merseyside *(Lancastria)*
172

Norfolk *(Norfolcia)*
24, 43, 84, 183

North Yorkshire *(Eboracum)*
17, 23, 29, 44, 79, 130, 166, 174

Northumberland *(Northumbria)*
95, 98, 99, 141

Oxfordshire *(Oxonium)*
18, 56, 60, 64, 77, 100, 101, 108, 111,
113, 116, 146, 149, 151, 156, 157, 162,
185, 187, 188, 191

Shropshire *(Salopia)*
61

Somerset *(Somersetus)*
22, 39, 90

Suffolk *(Suffolcia)*
153

Surrey *(Surria)*
143

Tyne and Wear
(Dunelmesis epis)
54

Warwickshire *(Warwic)*
82, 92, 110, 132, 138, 168, 189

West Midlands *(Warwic)*
25, 103

Wiltshire *(Wiltonia)*
70, 93

Index